GW00371100

SETTING

The nature and the outcome of therapy are always to some extent determined by the way the therapist decides to conduct the initial session. In *Setting Out* Lesley Murdin and Meg Errington explore the issues surrounding this subject, providing valuable insights into the significance of beginnings in psychotherapy.

The book deals with practical issues for the therapist, such as the responsibility for the unfolding of the therapeutic relationship. It also addresses ethical and technical debates over how much should be said at the initial meeting, and how the beginning can determine the outcome. Subjects covered include:

- The birth of a narrative self
- Diagnosis: should we even begin?
- Expectations: the birth of pattern recognition
- Transference: the birth of the problem of reality
- Countertransference

Illustrated throughout with case vignettes and fully referenced for further study, this exploration of the crucial issue of how to manage beginnings will prove to be an invaluable resource for students of counselling and psychotherapy as well as experienced practitioners.

SETTING OUT

The importance of the beginning in psychotherapy and counselling

Lesley Murdin with Meg Errington

Routledge
Taylor & Francis Group

LONDON AND NEW YORK

First published 2005 by Routledge
27 Church Road, Hove, East Sussex BN3 2FA

Simultaneously published in the USA and Canada
By Routledge
270 Madison Avenue, New York, NY 10016

Routledge is an imprint of the Taylor & Francis Group

© 2005 Lesley Murdin with Meg Errington

Typeset in Times by Garfield Morgan, Rhayader, Powys
Printed and bound in Great Britain by TJ International Ltd, Padstow, Cornwall
Paperback cover design by Sandra Heath

This publication has been produced with paper manufactured to strict
environmental standards and with pulp derived from sustainable forests.

British Library Cataloguing in Publication Data
A catalogue record for this book is available from the British Library

Library of Congress Cataloging-in-Publication Data
Murdin, Lesley.
Setting out : the importance of the beginning in psychotherapy and
counselling / by Lesley Murdin with Meg Errington.
p. cm.
Includes bibliographical references and index.
ISBN 1-58391-934-1 (hbk.) – ISBN 1-58391-935-X (pbk.)
1. Psychotherapist and patient. 2. Psychotherapy. 3.
Psychoanalysis.
I. Errington, Meg. II. Title.

RC480.8.M87 2005
616.89'14–dc21
2004015983

ISBN 1-58391-934-1 (hbk)
ISBN 1-58391-935-X (pbk)

This book is dedicated to
Ben Churchill.
He taught us much of what we know.

CONTENTS

PREFACE

As with the therapeutic relationship, so also with writing a book: much had happened before I started. I had already taken up a position within the various debates about the nature of psycho-analysis and psychotherapy. Except when quoting someone else, I speak of the *patient*, the one who suffers, rather than the *client,* with its overtones from the Latin origin of the word *cliens* implying the dependent who seeks patronage from the power of a patron. I do not like that implication. Nor do I like the later sense of the word, which has come to imply the recipient of a commercial transaction.

Whatever my intentions, I have to accept that the use of *psychoanalysis, psychoanalytic psychotherapy* and *patient* will locate me in a certain position which may be alien to some members of the profession. I have also chosen to use the female pronouns for the therapist and the masculine for the patient. This is partly a political statement and partly I think an accurate reflection of the fact that the majority of psychotherapists and counsellors are women. Psychoanalysts, psychotherapists and counsellors are all referred to as *analysts* or *clinicians*.

My view that the primary task of therapeutic work is analysis will also alienate some of the profession. The task that interests me is that of self-examination to achieve better internal and external relating. This may or may not lead to greater happiness, but, following Socrates and, I believe, most of the philosophers, I subscribe to the view that the unexamined life is not worth living. I am not a philosopher but I am influenced by the writing of twentieth-century philosophers, particularly the implication for morality of the stream of thought about the essence of being that flows through Heidegger, Foucault and Levinas. By this I do not mean the endless round of self-analysis often dismissed as 'navel gazing', but taking up a broad view of the whole of one's existence in relation to immediate perceptions. In other words, I pose to myself and others questions about the meaning and value of existence.

These are in themselves perhaps matters of taste or opinion but together they will add up to an author whom the reader will begin to assess as alien or acceptable. I hope that by addressing the effect that these qualities might have on the reader I will have enabled us to form some sort of working relationship.

Lesley Murdin

ACKNOWLEDGEMENTS

I would like to thank the following for help and encouragement: Paul Murdin, Benita Kyle and Colette Levy.

1

IN THE BEGINNING WAS THE WORD

The beginning is not the beginning. When a person first meets a psychotherapist, a great deal has already happened. The two people involved in adult individual therapy or analysis have histories, hopes and desires, and the patient is not the only one with more going on in his mind than is conscious. In fact the direction of the relationship may already have been set by the referral process, even before the two people have met.

That is not to say that the direction of the relationship cannot be changed. It does mean that it has a trajectory which can be changed by a deliberate effort. In other words, part of the duty of the therapist is to understand what has happened already. She must think consciously and as far as possible she must delve into the unconscious processes both in herself and her patient, and into the new creations from the mix of both. She must do this before and during the first meeting.

In writing of beginnings I am aware that I am imposing an order on a process which is without limits. The desire to make finitude is defensive in that it helps us to avoid our fear of infinity. At the same time our therapeutic finitudes enable theory to be made and debated and we would be poorer without the sheer enjoyment of theory, however psychotic it may be to seek to encompass the human mind in ideas that can be articulated and tamed through language.

Freud himself believed in beginnings. He completed the *Interpretation of Dreams* in 1888 but made sure that it was published with the date of 1900. It mattered to him to be right in at the beginning of the twentieth century, not the very end of the nineteenth. During the twentieth century, psychoanalysis lost its air of newness and while its practitioners still debate its premises with great vigour, in the wider academic world criticism of the

1

arts, sociology and psychology takes its fundamental ideas for granted.

Nevertheless, there is life in the conceptual framework and in the clinical practice of psychoanalysis and there is room for further new beginning in the twenty-first century. I intend in this book to develop some ideas derived from the study of psychoanalysis itself and from the influence of neuroscience and genetics.

Any analytic practitioner working today must be aware of the tension between the valuing of the ego and its ability to choose a path for the individual, and the knowledge that every conscious intention may be subverted by the unconscious. The psychotherapist who holds any view of the mind similar to this must approach the beginning of work with a new patient with the awareness of the inconspicuous Other (of either of the two people in the room) who may try to shipwreck the boat currently sailing across calm water. Paradoxically, the Other may sometimes be glimpsed in the first meeting, often the merest flicker of fins, as the fish repeatedly disappears beneath the surface.

Approaching a therapist can be a major step for anyone. Perhaps in the USA it is easier than in the culture of the UK. In both countries, it may be easier to do at the beginning of the twenty-first century than it has been in the past. But nowhere and never will it be easy to enter therapy. It requires courage and faith. At some level there must be a wish for a new beginning. For some, it is a simple matter of desperation. Nothing could be worse than their present suffering and just possibly a therapist could help.

I take the position that the beginning of therapy is of vital importance for several reasons. Many potential patients attend for only one session and then do not return. What do they take away with them? For those who stay for psychotherapy or counselling, the course that is set in the early sessions may determine how much they can achieve. Most of us would agree that the therapist's most important role in the early sessions is to listen attentively and actively. Many concerns and many aspects of the process itself can make this difficult and I intend in this book to address the ways in which the therapist may be diverted from paying attention to the essential nature of the patient in front of her.

If it is difficult to attend the first session, how difficult is it to return for another session after the first? Little can be promised. We cannot yet show that any one model of therapy has generally better outcomes than any other. Each therapist has to assess whether her own model will help or harm this particular patient. So why does anyone ever return for another session when so little certain can be said? There is a point at which the person is ready to become a patient. The psychoanalytic aphorism says that he must be sick enough to need therapy and healthy enough to stand it. A degree of health in some part of the psyche must be invoked for anyone to tolerate the frustrations and pain of long-term work.

From the point of view of the patient, much depends on the referral. Some areas of suffering are now generally recognised to deserve therapeutic intervention. Specific tasks may be given to a counsellor who is asked to work with a patient who has, for example, been told that he has a life-threatening condition such as cancer or HIV infection. The task might be considered to be: 'help him come to terms with it'. We do not know what that means for any individual. In some cases, the popular use of the phrase may place an obligation on the patient to appear to return to normality after a brief period when he is allowed to be seen to suffer. Jane Haynes and Juliet Miller (2003) have published a text on the effects of infertility and the need for therapeutic intervention in the case where a woman is using assisted reproductive technology (ART). Their useful collection of papers demonstrates that natural conception through the intercourse of a man and a woman is regarded by many as not only a right of human beings but also an obligation. Those who for some reason are unable to conceive are likely to feel shame or guilt as well as the pain and deprivation of their childless state.

The novelist Hilary Mantel (2003) suffered from severe endometriosis, which damages the uterus, and had to have a hysterectomy. The medical staff involved defended themselves against the understanding of what this might mean for her by referring to what was removed as *clinical waste*:

> If the chain that links you to biological destiny is severed, you are left winded and bruised on the road, the casualty in an accident. You come up hard against the question: what's the use of me? At the date when I was carried into the op theatre I was ambivalent about whether I should have children and I always had been . . . The impact of childlessness for me has been subtle and long delayed. But the issue of infertility confronted me as soon as my stitches had been taken out.
>
> (Mantel 2003: 21)

Mantel is speaking of the sense that there is a right to happiness. If we are missing something, we must find out what it is and acquire it; then all will be well. Often the achievement of analytic therapy has to be the articulation of desire and the acceptance of a position which may not include having one's heart's desire. The clinician will be aware of the cultural and personal templates of the contentment and safety that existed before the 'Fall' or the exodus from Paradise.

Haynes and Miller (2003) make clear that this template is present for men as well as for women. Raphael Leff (2003: 34) writes that 'a meeting of grasping vagina and thrusting penis depositing bodily fluid inside her may invoke symbolic parallels with the milk filled nipple and sucking mouth of breast feeding'. If this is the case, we would have reason to think that the beginning of life is of symbolic importance not only to women of reproductive age, but to both sexes and to people of all ages.

For some people the hope that the therapist seems to offer is the ability to accept that one's current life is not being wasted. Freedom to be one's self brings with it guilt. Mick Cooper (2003), in describing the basis of existential psychotherapy, refers to Heidegger ([1927] 1963) in relation to the guilt that is equivalent to remorse for all the opportunities that one has wasted: 'Taking up relationships in the world is possible only through acceptance of *Dasein* as Being-in-the-world as it is' ([1927] 1963: 89). Those who do not accept their concrete existence in the world (*Dasein*) in relation to others will live only in part. Existential therapists are particularly well placed to hear the disappointment that most of us have in varying degrees but which is to be faced if life is to be lived as well as it can be.

For most people, the underlying presenting problem can be traced to some sort of loss and it is for comfort or a solution to loss that they look. They may need to see the symbolic implications of current relationships in terms of their own originary myth. A useful question for the assessment procedure might be: how do you think your parents felt about your birth? Each patient will have his own myth, often unconscious about his own beginning. When this myth is expressed in words it can be subject to change and to the effects of subsequent experience. The therapy itself is likely to create an attitude in the patient to his own desirability. All the therapist need do is say or imply 'See you next week.'

When the clinician begins the process of therapy, she will to some extent retrace the process of beginning to relate to others.

4

Have we a template for the origin of any human mind? Philosophy gives us questions about existence but merely enjoins us to observe it through the processes of phenomenology: 'Phenomenology means to let that which shows itself be seen from itself' (Heidegger [1927] 1963: 62). Psychoanalysis has some difficulty in restricting itself to phenomena. At least we might try to begin from what shows itself and we can take our task as being in part to watch what has shown itself unfolding.

Each model of therapy has some sort of developmental story. Freud gave us the theory of fixation points and some justification for the jargon of 'being stuck', and even worse, the invention of the noun 'stuckness'. Carl Jung presented posterity with the possibility of hard-wired predispositions for relationships in the concept of the archetype, and has left subsequent generations to puzzle over what exactly he meant. Recent writers have developed their own descriptions of the archetype (Papadopoulos and Saayman 1984; Samuels 1985). Jean Knox (2003: 30) has made a most thorough investigation of the possible confusion, dating back to Jung himself, over the meanings of the concept:

- Biological entities in the form of information which is hard-wired in the genes, providing a set of instructions to the mind as well as the body.
- Organising mental frameworks of an abstract nature, a set of rules or instructions but with no symbolic or representational content so that they are never directly experienced.
- Core meanings which do contain representational content and which therefore provide a central symbolic significance to our experience.
- Metaphysical entities which are eternal and are therefore independent of the body.

Knox concludes that the most fruitful understanding of the archetype comes from a reading of the information that we can now take from genetics. The gene conveys a message which focuses the attention of the developing child. We are acquiring the understanding that the information contained in the human genome is not sufficient to form any kind of template for a human being, but is instead able to act as a catalyst: 'The gene as a catalyst is highly interactive with the environment . . . a mechanism for focusing attention onto specific perceptual patterns' (Knox 2003: 20). The gene seems to do this in many animals.

5

These patterns can be stored in a simple schematised form which then allows all similar patterns to be recognised. Knox then goes on to consider the development of the human infant, in terms of the activation of pattern recognition. For example, the newborn infant has been shown to be more interested in patterns that resemble a human face than in any other shapes or designs:

> This response is not intentional or social, it is in fact a sensory-motor response: It should be clear that we believe that young infants orient to faces under the guidance of a sensory motor reflex: the new-born does not require to understand 'the meaning' of a face.
>
> (Knox 2003: 50)

Knox is clear that the concept of an archetype as some form of structuring or patterning predisposition must be kept distinct from the content which we might distinguish as the archetypal image. This viewpoint implies that the patient comes to therapy with some sort of patterning responses built into his approach to a new situation. The content will be supplied by the process of therapy itself. Some of the expectancies created by the patterning will be filled by new experiences and may be less toxic than in the past. Others will be given content for the first time. In subsequent chapters I shall examine the ways in which the initial stage of therapy may make use of this capacity or may be damaged by it. The therapist who wishes to be competent, and to give the patient the best experience possible, clearly needs to be informed about the developments of information theory as well as genetics and neuroscience. This is not an easy prescription to fill.

The British object relations school and the attachment theorists have also given us ways of thinking of the developmental processes as a beginning. In the experiments of Harlow (1958), for example, baby monkeys who were offered a choice between a wire mother with a feeding bottle and a soft, cloth mother without a bottle chose to spend most of their time with the soft, cloth mother. One implication for the therapist is that no matter how effectively she offers nutrition, this will not be acceptable unless she allows for the need to cling to what is soft for at least some of the time. Object relations theory takes as a major premise that the human infant seeks object relations above all else and that it is frustration in this seeking that leads to aggression and all evil.

This is a view that takes human nature as essentially good and redeemable in spite of the misfortunes and rejections encountered along the way.

Kleinian analysts, who take the view that a great deal is already given in the human infant at birth even before the processes of introjection and projection set about firming up the innate tendencies, must find some way of believing that there is still scope for changing the nature of the internal objects. All therapists must use their own version of theory in such a way that they can usefully think about patients and can have hope for improvement in their mental state. For this reason, it is an ethical obligation for therapists to read and debate and achieve a thorough understanding of whatever theory they use so that they can be confident that they have addressed the pitfalls and will still be able to keep enough faith. In that sense too, each new patient demands a new beginning for the clinician.

This leads to the necessity of examining the therapist's own myth of the beginning of her own life. She must watch the way in which it interacts with the patient's previous experience. Could she be trying to repair her own myth through a patient? Some of the bad ways to begin are obvious. The person who is sent for counselling to an agency responsible for a particular area such as adoption or ART is likely to be given a very short series of sessions, most often three or six. These sessions can be very useful but can also re-create the experience of the adopted child who is supplanted by the next baby whom the mother then loves and desires more. Some therapists are very careful not to take on several new patients one after the other because there is the risk that the patient will sense being no longer the apple of mother's eye before being ready to endure this deprivation.

In private practice, patients are usually self-referred in the sense that they do not arrive with a letter of referral. They may have obtained the name of a practitioner from a friend or relative. This kind of personal reference gives the practitioner a good chance that the initial feelings will be positive.

A potential patient is given my name by a patient who is ending her own therapy. The prospective patient telephones me, saying, 'I've heard that you are the best. I will wait as long as necessary if I can get to see you. I am not going to see anyone else.' Of course I hear this with mixed feelings. I think first of all

7

of the patient who is leaving and his need to give me a gift and perhaps to be vicariously present in the room with the new patient. When I think of the new person, I am aware that expectations will be very high and that there seems to be an idealisation which is going to be maintained with some fervour. I will of course need to meet with the new person for an assessment interview and I make no assumption that either he or I will wish to begin his analysis after that.

This situation is representative of therapies in which someone approaches a practitioner who has a reputation, perhaps derived from published material or from personal recommendation. In either case, the potential patient is led by need or even by envy to seek a parent figure, who will be able and perhaps willing to be idealised for a while. Kohut (1965) is emphatic that the practitioner must allow some idealisation. Jones (2002) points out that philosophers such as Durkheim and Fromm have emphasised the value of idealisation in a process of transformation (p. 79). This is a logical corollary of the mirroring theories of Lacan and Winnicott. If the small child derives his image of himself from the mirror or from the metaphorical mirror in his mother's eyes, we would have to assume that the practitioner needs to allow some time in which the image being enjoyed is of the ideal, wise, knowledgeable individual who does not exist in the other chair, but whose fantasised existence may be assimilated by the patient, if it is not destroyed by the therapist too soon.

Jacques Lacan (1949) viewed the assimilation of the mirror image as the prototype of a vast area of *méconnaissance,* or misunderstanding in the ego. The small child sees his own image in the mirror but mistakes it for an image with power and physical beauty and ability. He cannot tell yet that the image adds nothing to the reality of his weakness and limitation. Any therapist who is sobered by Lacan's critique will in any case be aware that all her own interpretations of the patient's perceptions may be subject to the same limitations and mistaken assumptions.

The value of re-experiencing the illusion, or *méconnaissance,* is great, because the practitioner has the opportunity to enable the patient to come to understand the danger of over-relying on any perception or interpretation. In fact, the patient is faced with the task of trusting the clinician enough to talk to her but also not to expect too much of her. The initial hope may well be unreasonable

8

and idealistic. She may tolerate it to begin with to some extent, but has the responsibility of not encouraging it.

One aspect of idealisation is the notion of *cure*, which may develop as a *folie à deux* beckoning both patient and clinician: 'The notion of cure and putting right is a regressive one, a mutual transference fantasy of great pathos but negative therapeutic value, which identifies the therapist as a magical rescuer and covers up the trauma again in the act of exposing it' (Totton 2002: 19). Nick Totton is here speaking specifically of body psychotherapy, but his emphasis on the initial idealisation of psychotherapy itself is relevant across the different models. Charles Rycroft (1968) pointed out the importance of disillusionment, which is necessary but should not be catastrophic. In this he referred to the thinking of Winnicott (1965) who emphasised the need for the patient's therapist, like the parent, to achieve a gradual, tolerable failure:

> A mother who cannot gradually fail in this matter of sensitive adaptation is failing in another sense, she is failing because of her own immaturity or her own anxieties to give her infant reasons for anger. An infant that has no reason for anger but who of course has in him or her the usual amount of whatever are the ingredients of aggressiveness is in a special difficulty, a difficulty in fusing aggression in with loving.
>
> (Winnicott 1965: 87)

Failure must be caught by an environment which provides enough safety for it to be tolerable. The beginning of the therapy will either unfold this possibility or risk not achieving it at all. To some extent the patient's expectations will determine what the chances are (see Chapter 5).

The therapist then prepares an environment in which there is the possibility of addressing some of what has been hidden from the patient himself. The direction of the treatment will also depend on the readiness of the person to enter and bring with him the environment that has been holding him in his cultural and social context.

Attitudes to analysis will be embedded in the social and cultural context of any individual. In the UK, at the beginning of the twenty-first century, there are many parodies. Peter Sellers in the film *What's New, Pussycat?* portrayed a psychotherapist in a red velvet suit, a caricature, presenting the wish of the outsider that the therapist would prove to be a useless neurotic whose services no one would need. The film *Analyse This* depicts the psychotherapist as the helpless and vulnerable (though well-meaning) civilian caught up in the forces of the underworld in a way which threatens to overwhelm him. Other American films have mostly presented the serious psychotherapist as the doctor in his office, sitting behind a huge desk writing notes, while the patient struggles alone on a couch somewhere at the other side of the room. This is difficult to recognise from the point of view of an ordinary working practitioner who sits in a chair similar to that of the patient, or beside the couch, and would not dream of writing notes to distract her from her intensive listening to what the patient is communicating.

The press and media in general in the UK at the beginning of the twenty-first century are very negative about the psychological therapies. Reasons for this might be connected with the privacy of the relationship and the material that evolves in the consulting room. Journalists are disposed to like transparency, or at least the option of a good story. When dealing with our profession they come up against the inevitable ethical prohibition against speaking about one's patients. In my experience it might be possible to have much more positive media coverage of our work if we were able to give stories of actual treatments and photographs of happy patients. As it is, the stories tend to be about the few unsatisfied patients who wish to tell their stories themselves. Sometimes there is research which provides an opportunity for journalists to write about the contrast between pharmacological treatment and the outcomes expected from psychological therapy, which is bound to be longer and less easy to measure reliably in either its positive or negative effects.

Experience is beginning to show that one session of counselling is not helpful and could even be harmful in the case of severe trauma, such as a train crash. This is a beginning which may well be offered too soon in some cases, a possibility well understood in the responsible part of the profession. Patients must be allowed to make their own way through the early stages of trauma and to ask for therapy if they are unable to move on or if they feel that they will benefit from being able to speak with someone with professional expertise who is uninvolved. The Sunday papers make a meal of the idea that counsellors prevent people from recovering from trauma by persuading them to go over and over a terrible event. This may be so in a few cases but the truth is that we see people who have not been able to process an event and are suffering from being unable to forget it. We might, in some cases of dissociation, phobia or obsession, help the patient to remember in order to be able to forget. If a person could manage perfectly well without us, we would be surprised to see him more than once or twice.

The popular media are right in one respect, however. Therapy is dangerous in the same measure that it is powerful. Once a person has chosen analytic therapy and embarked on a serious intention to make changes with the help of a therapist, processes are set in train which may make it difficult to end. Human beings are capable of all sorts of evil but they are also capable of love. Loving a therapist is not a bad thing. There are many different ways of loving as most people already know. Love that comes from gratitude and is connected to a desire to know something of the other person's mind and feelings will make a person more connected to life and to constructive parts of himself. On the other hand, love that is excessively narcissistic can tip over into obsession or demand and the therapist may be faced with a kind of stalking which is particularly difficult to manage. Therapists suffer from pursuit, often by telephone calls and messages. In the most extreme cases their families may be threatened and endangered. In such cases the therapist has only the usual protection from the law that any citizen has and in general must rely on professional skill to defuse the powerful emotions which have so much of both hate and love in them.

Leaving the therapist will be difficult for some people, even if much of the hate has been transformed into love and the love that remains is the correlate of gratitude. The more infantile forms of love will make ending impossible without some sort of catastrophe. Nevertheless, however difficult the situation that they produce, these forms of love are the essential material of psychotherapy and no clinician can expect to avoid dealing with them as the very stuff of the work that must be done.

I have said that these are infantile forms of love. This is based on the theoretical viewpoint that connects pathology with a developmental metaphor. People whose love is very demanding and all-consuming, who want to 'eat up' the object of love, can be said to remain at the stage of development that Freud and Klein (1959) depicted as oral. Eating precedes speech as the baby puts everything in his mouth before he can ask questions or express his fear or his love in words. Those who stick to obsessive ritual or maintain a phobic distance can be thought of as remaining at the anal stage and would in this view have to make changes which are equivalent to progressing in developmental terms. The ultimate stage of developmental achievement is the genital stage, which can be seen as the point at which love can develop into a more adult relation to the other, leading to a possibly creative or fruitful intercourse. Once this intercourse is achieved, there is the possibility of parting and this is the distinguishing sadness of the therapeutic relationship; unlike any other human relationship, it is begun with the clear assumption on both sides that it must end through the choice of one of the parties.

Most of the people who present for psychological therapy do so because their ability to love is blocked in some way. On the surface this may present as a loss of some sort. The patient may present a fairly clear picture of one of the gross areas of pathology, fitting Freud's description of the neuroses. Or it may be that he is mourning the loss of a love, which did reach the level of a genital relationship but which has been taken away by some sort of disaster, not always death. Nevertheless, each person will need to show the worst difficulties in relating while in the session with the therapist. We can then label the painful response that the therapist might feel as the effect of regressive behaviour from the patient. One of the important criteria for beginning therapy will be the degree of potential regression, which will affect the extent to which it can be managed. A patient who will allow no acknowledgment of regression will be unlikely to benefit from analytic therapy.

Assuming that the patient and clinician agree to work together, they enter the beginning phase of the work. The patient usually tries his best to tell the practitioner in words and in behaviour what has brought him to her. He will also have reservations: those things that are too shameful to tell and which he can easily persuade himself are not necessary for her to know. Beyond the words, much will happen that is below the level of conscious thought. Body language will make an impact. Tones of voice will add to the meaning of what is actually said. Questions are posed unconsciously, answers absorbed and attitudes adopted, often without conscious awareness. Is the practitioner interested in dreams or in sex or in people with difficulties or only in people who can solve their own problems quickly? Practitioners who remain alert can make from this beginning a valuable agenda for the work that needs to be done.

So far I have spoken mainly about the beginning of the therapy from the clinician's point of view. Chapter 5 will examine the expectations that shape the encounter for both patient and therapist. Prospective patients are usually not naive. They often do some research on what they can expect from psychotherapy or analysis. They come with demands and quite reasonably wish to know whether they can be helped by a given therapist.

Unfortunately, few therapists have very clear ideas about just how much a given model of therapy is going to be able to help a given patient. Most clinicians accept the need for evidence-based practice, but 'evidence' is often no more than intuition. We might be able to say that we do not expect that a person will be able to use a verbal therapy or tolerate the frustration and deprivation that might be involved, but studies of outcomes are still not adequate in making definitive statements. In any case, individuals can still surprise us and we should give up doing this work if we no longer recognise that hope can be found even where there seems to be none. Nevertheless, every practitioner should be prepared to recognise when another model might be of more use than her own. For example, individually trained psychotherapists need to be able to recognise when a group analysis might be beneficial or when cognitive techniques might be more useful than analysis.

So far I have written as though the clinician is alone with the patient and her theoretical model. This should not be the case. Every responsible therapist should have a consultant or supervisor and should make her work visible to someone else. Often a trusted colleague as supervisor or consultant can provide the external view that is needed, most of all regarding the decision about whether or not to take on a patient in the first place, because colleagues know each other's strengths and weaknesses better than anyone else can. There is also a body of knowledge coming from research both outside and within the discipline of psychoanalysis which can help to make the endeavour more focused, more likely to be helpful and less idiosyncratic.

Researchers have paid some attention to the beginning of psychotherapy because it is the point from which outcomes can be measured. In other words, the beginning is interesting because it is the beginning of the end. In order to make any assessment of change during psychoanalysis or psychotherapy, the researchers must find a baseline from which to measure. The baseline will, in most cases, be a statement of the goals that the patient took for his therapy or it will be a description of the symptoms that were brought to the beginning of the therapy.

One study by Beutel and Rousting (2002: 134) relied on retrospective questionnaires to establish the initial conditions for the treatment. On average, treatments had been terminated six and a half years before the follow-up study took place. Patients were asked to report on their state before treatment began and to estimate the improvement (if any) that they would ascribe to the analysis. The treating therapists were also asked for their view of the change that took place. Memories of what had brought patients to see a therapist tended to be of broad areas of symptoms such as 'chronic back pain'. This patient remembered enough to assess the change that she had experienced: 'I have developed a feeling for me, for my needs and particularly for the limits of my capability . . . I gained a positive access to my own gender' (Beutel and Rousting 2002: 135). In the patient's assessment of the value of the therapy, there is no mention of the symptom with which she began it. Beutel and Rousting refer to the symptom as not being the only or major factor in the patients' assessments: 'Former patients did not only take the presence or absence of symptoms into account but also their means of coping with symptoms' (2002: 136).

The idea of the symptom as the badge that entitles a person to analysis or some form of psychological treatment is important both to the potential patient and to the therapist. There are few published studies that demonstrate the context and subjective reasons why people enter analysis. Rosemary Dinnage (1988) interviewed a number of people at various stages of analysis and psychotherapy. She shows us how the prospective patient needs to feel that it is acceptable to attend sessions and to be known to be 'in analysis'. Some may follow friends or relatives: 'I had two close friends who qualified at the same time as me and they both went into psychiatry' (1988: 31). Alex followed these friends 'into analysis'. Aimlessness itself enabled Alex to begin analysis without having to have an aim. Many people need the surface evidence of a problem that a symptom implies; symptoms are externally visible signifiers of the hidden inner problem which is going to take weeks, months or years to discover. The symptom itself is that which can be shown without words or put into words that only obscure the reason for the symptom's existence. In cases taken on for counselling, the symptom tends to be an external problem or life difficulty which can be described more or less clearly in words. In psychotherapy and psychoanalysis the symptom is likely to be a neurotic, psychotic or perverse formation. Nevertheless, it has a structure. An achievement of the therapy may be that it becomes possible to express the meaning in words.

The emphasis on symptoms in psychological treatment demonstrates the extent to which psychoanalysis and its derivatives have been influenced by the medical model and yet have departed from it into a different form of understanding: 'The symptom is intelligible to the psychotherapist as exemplifying an aimful situation' (Saks 2001: 23). Everyone knows that you cannot expect much from a doctor if you show up in his surgery and say 'There's nothing wrong with me, doctor.' There has to be something wrong if you are to be any concern of the doctor's, even if it is simply that you are unhappy. Most general practitioners (GPs) in the UK employ counsellors with varying levels of training and personal therapy in their own background to whom they would refer such a patient, usually for a brief period of supportive work. They might also consider anti-depressants and/or a psychiatric referral if they thought it appropriate.

On the other hand, many people who attend a clinic for psychoanalysis or psychotherapy also say in effect that they are unhappy. This could constitute a symptom, as it is cut off from conscious awareness of its roots. The therapist's task is to look for the unconscious correlates of the unhappiness. As the patient talks we will no doubt discover that there are effects in relationships, in work effectiveness, perhaps also minor physical symptoms, all of which can be connected to the efforts of the central problem to get itself noticed.

Diagnosis is the subject of Chapter 3 and will be considered in more depth there.

Before the first meeting there must be a first telephone call followed by crossing the threshold into the room for the first time. New trainees need to be reminded of the significance of the first voice greeting, which is often an answerphone message. In private practice, there may be other family members who are allowed to answer the telephone, and messages may be left by a voice other than that of the practitioner. In clinic situations it may be possible to choose whether the voice that is heard first is that of a man or a woman. Opinion is divided about which is best for the majority of patients. In all cases clarity and perhaps some warmth will help the patient to overcome the difficulty of the initial telephone call.

Recognition of the anxiety of the patient which may express itself in demands or elusiveness helps both patient and therapist. Many practitioners will recognise the patient who wants to know exactly what kind of therapy you are offering, how long it will take and what the outcome will be. Of course, none of these questions can be answered except in very general terms over the telephone, before an initial meeting. Some therapists now seek to obviate such questions by putting a statement on their website. As a profession, we have to be prepared to say *something* and to take responsibility for our implied promises.

Chapter 4 will look at the questions raised in forming a contractual agreement with the patient. The first moments of contact will have an effect on the patient's hopes and fears and on the extent to which they can manage their demands, needs and desires. Nini Herman (1988) describes her experience with therapists from each of the three main streams of analysis: Jungian, Freudian and finally Kleinian. Herman described her first meeting with her Jungian therapist: 'A motherly small personage in a vaguely eastern dress bade me follow her upstairs. Ageless, timeless, effortless, she floated ahead of me . . . Two chairs were standing face to face among the many books and plants that were thriving everywhere' (1988: 61–2). Much might occur to the reader as a message to the potential patient in such a setting. We could allow for some of the writer's literary skill in conveying much through small detail, but we have to remember that we all become experts in reading certain types of text and where something as important as the first encounter with a therapist is concerned, there is bound to be a heightened level of awareness.

A Jungian would usually wish to have two chairs rather than a couch. This is to imply a fundamental equality which, of course, the whole situation belies: 'Three times a week I went along and sat obediently in her chair because, it seemed, she wanted that. I intended to do everything exactly as she wished and be no trouble. It was kind of her to let me come considering how bad I was' (Herman 1988: 63). Every patient is anxious to see how much his therapist knows and how authoritative she is willing to be. Whatever the illness or need of the patient, the unspoken cry is, 'Tell me how to get better. I don't know and I hope to God that you do.'

Patients therefore enter the room with a predisposition to see hopeful signs as well as with a cynical determination in many cases to find all the reasons not to be able to hope. Nini Herman might have been able to find encouragement in the thriving of the plants and books. At least this woman can look after plants. She might also have taken the 'vaguely eastern dress' to imply some sort of wisdom and knowledge beyond the ordinary. In fact, Herman reached a position where she could see for herself with hindsight her need for the infantile feelings and transferences to be analysed. The kind of Jungian analysis that spoke to the adult in intellectual terms had also provided her with elements of good mothering which she clearly recognised: 'She had never let me down. I had always found her kind and even tempered, never harsh, preoccupied or punitive from which I must have drawn some image of a mother with whom I could identify' (Herman 1988: 74). Such important aspects of any analysis are not immediately apparent and may never be consciously recognised by the patient, but are present in the general acceptance that this is a place to which I can bear to return and where I shall be welcomed.

Herman's second analysis illustrates a different sort of problem that can appear in the first session encounter. She was able to deceive her Freudian therapist into accepting her own version of herself as a competent adult: he 'had simply no idea that he had been entrusted with the pieces of a splintered child. She had come to him disguised as a mother, wife and doctor'. Nevertheless, the first encounter had promised well. He had the ambience of the 'wise old man' which linked him helpfully to her Jungian experience. He was 'the spitting image of an ancient Highland laird'. His 'courteous manner and warming smile drew me to him instantly' (1988: 100). The analysis never became useful to the splintered child and Herman herself blames a lack of analysis of the child transference. Neither her love nor her hate was analysed and the feelings cavorted unchecked. Moreover she felt that she was able to induce in her therapist a 'crisis of confidence' (1988: 101), which of course terrified her all the more and no doubt induced further acting out and in.

The third analysis was the Kleinian and this time everything was just right. One can draw conclusions about the models but probably much relates to the individual therapists concerned. The third, Dr G., had no pretensions to any trappings: 'Even the window boxes had very little more than weeds' (Herman 1988: 114). The plate outside the door had no letters after the name, just the plain name itself. Dr G.'s first intervention was similarly unpretentious. He said: 'So you have had quite a hard time.' Herman found this simplicity, with the empathy that it conveyed, an immense relief.

Herman returns us to the few things that we know for certain about the effect of psychotherapy and its specialisms of counselling and psychoanalysis. There is no need for luxurious consulting rooms. There is no need for new techniques to shock the patient, nor for cups of coffee to encourage euphoria. What is needed is what we always knew would count: an ability to listen with care and benevolence and an ability to respect love and use the word.

This patient, speaking to Dinnage (1988: 18), certainly knew this: 'You see I had reached one three dimensional god awful full stop. You see it was a black hole that I fell into and I went on and on and down and down'.

Some people arrive in therapy out of a sense of emptiness or aimlessness: 'I think I was aware at some level that there was something very wrong with my life. I had a sense of aimlessness, feelings of futility. I suppose I knew that there was a future waiting for me that I wasn't going to be able to accommodate to' (Dinnage 1988: 32).

The first encounter must show that the therapist can bear this, even if it shows little else. Then there is a chance that the patient and therapist together may find for the patient the future that he *can* bear.

2

THE BIRTH OF A
NARRATIVE SELF

Full speech is speech which aims at, which forms, the truth
such as it becomes established in the recognition of one
person by another. Full speech is speech which performs.
One of the subjects finds himself other than he was before.

(Lacan 1955: 107)

Art is a lie that makes us realise truth, at least the truth
that is given us to understand.

(Pablo Picasso quoted in Barr 1946)

In my work with adolescents, I have become interested in what I
have come to think of as the emergence of a 'narrative' self. All
English teachers of first-year pupils at secondary school are
familiar with this notion and one of the most frequent first schemes
of work set in English lessons will often be a unit called 'Myself' or
'My autobiography' or some such, in an attempt to foster a narrative self. The child at the end of latency, aged 11 or 12, who is often
least equipped to expand on his experience and is happiest reading
children's novels like the *Harry Potter* series is encouraged at the
point of transition from primary to secondary school to chronicle
the significant moments and experiences of his history, something
many children find difficult. They are embedded in their lives and
cannot easily at this point in their development stand outside of
themselves to self-observe as required. They do not see themselves
as having a history. Many of the adolescents I see for psychotherapy have great difficulty in beginning to tell me their life story,

19

often passively waiting for me to do the work for them and tell them about themselves. More seriously, they are unable to suspend their action-dominated, impulsive selves to begin to tell me the things in their lives which they probably have tried very hard to play down or forget. Sometimes parents are brought in, in the early stages of the work, to tell their version of events and help the therapist out with a plausible narrative coherence and a framework from which to begin.

Many of these difficulties are of course reflected in work with adult patients. The diagnostic test known as the Adult Attachment Interview is a method of discovering the adult's ability to tell a coherent story about himself and as a result is a valuable diagnostic and research tool. In psychotherapy, we usually begin with a story and then go on to make revisions. According to the psychotherapist Gregory Bateson (1979: 13), we think in stories.

If psychotherapy is a 'talking cure' then it is essential to help the adolescent to talk and to go on talking, the aim with adolescents being the same as with adults: to encourage a playful, free association of thoughts and ideas. Problems with speaking and struggles with 'internalised language' which the psychologist Luria (1961) defines as thought itself, point to pathology in adolescence and can reveal profound difficulties in relating and communicating. According to Luria, it is through language we can control emotion and drives, because verbalisation of feelings makes it less necessary to enact them. We carry out self-management by inner speech or verbal thought (Luria 1961: 61). Peter Blos (1979: 282) writes in his classic work on adolescence, *The Adolescent Passage*, that 'The concreteness of action and of thing representation, their transition to symbolic speech and concept formation, represents a pivotal developmental point, on which hinges not only the individual mode of communication, but its progressive usefulness for adaptive mastery of the internal and external world'. Like Luria, Blos believes that language helps us to manage ourselves and to deal with the world. He has coined a notion of a 'concretising' adolescent, who uses the environment simultaneously for the gratification of infantile wishes and to extricate himself from needing to depend on others. All this echoes Freud, who in his 1905 paper 'The transformations of puberty' saw the task of puberty as the adolescent's ability to achieve 'active' mastery of his self rather than remaining in a state of 'passive' dependency (Freud 1905: 207). This, for Freud, was part of the adolescent's development towards mature sexual identity, coupled with the struggle to achieve ambivalence and 'the most painful psychic achievement of the pubertal period': detachment from parental authority. So listening to how adolescents speak and use language can tell us a great deal about where they are in terms of their development during this time. For Blos, 'concretisation' implies an inhibition in development, a continued passive dependence on the environment, rather than achieving what he refers to as 'the silent mastery of tension, through thought, fantasy, recollection and anticipation' (Blos 1979: 285). This limitation leads to impulsivity and a reliance on action as a tension regulator. This is inimical to insight which is rooted in introspection and contingent on internalisation and verbalised thought. For those working with adolescents all this is very familiar.

I worked recently with a 12-year-old girl, who had been referred ostensibly for grief counselling.

Jodie's grandfather had died, the only remaining member of the family her parents had any contact with, seeming to have fallen out with everyone. Jodie was very sad about her grandfather but matters were complicated by the fact that the family would inherit a significant amount of money on his death which meant that they could move out of their much hated council flat in London to France. Jodie was a highly intelligent girl, part of her school's programme for gifted and talented children, but what struck me was her difficulty at this stage of her life of challenging her parents' view of things which she tended to parrot in a passive way. Not only was London a dump and her school disappointing, she told me she was looking forward to eating a particular kind of cheese, a brie, made in the town they were moving to. She also mentioned enthusiastically a wine, brewed in the area. She had never tasted wine and it was as though she were repeating her parents' conversations piecemeal. This passivity was reflected in the way she read voraciously, often in her sessions. She told me she got into trouble for reading in class instead of doing her lessons. I wondered if she was reading so much to block out thoughts and feelings about her grandfather's death and the implications about leaving London and all her friends. She looked blankly at me as though I was mad. Who in their right mind would want to live in London if they could get out? However she stopped reading in sessions and began to write and draw. She would bring things for me to read out loud. First she started to write a Harry Potter novel of her own, again partly parodying and partly imitating the author's style which we could enjoy and discuss together and brought me in from out of the cold. Then she began to get interested in the bedroom she would have in her, much idealised, new home. She drew a picture of an elaborate room with red draperies, and old masters on the walls. Within that was a smaller room, 'with a key which my parents can't get at', she told me gleefully. Next session she brought a diary, with several detailed entries of worries about her mother and arguments she'd had with her, revealing how much she feared that her mother needed to be loved best and the difficulties she was having in forming attachments with others without upsetting her. This was very powerful to read – she wanted me to read it back to her, so that she could tell by my voice that I understood things. She often felt that her mother was too anxious to understand things. She told me she was going to continue to keep the diary when she moved. The diary had a lock. I was struck by the movement from a passive retreat through compulsive devouring of books into a much more active struggle to find language to express her fears and difficulties over the leaving of her old life and her separation from her mother. We had arrived at what Lacan would define as 'full speech'. This story would continue to generate meaning, not least in terms of her Oedipal struggle to love her father without fear of destroying her mother.

This was in contrast to John, a boy of the same age.

John was also part of his school's programme for gifted and talented children and he too defensively retreated into books. According to his teachers he wandered the corridors with books in his hands and after politely going through the motions with me for a few minutes in a session would with relief get out his book and bury himself in it, occasionally commenting on Orwell's use of irony in *Nineteen Eighty Four*, or reading me out a bit of Terry Pratchett. At times like that he talked to me like a pompous old man. At other times he idealised babyhood and passivity. He told me that the best thing was to be old because that was both being a baby and grown up and people puréed your food and 'you even have machines that help you breathe'. He couldn't find a way to tell me his story – he told me he didn't like chit chat – he could not give an account of himself. I had to piece things together from his mother and his teachers. He could not talk to me in any sustained way; after moments of meeting he would withdraw into a book and it is perhaps no surprise that he had few friends and was badly bullied by other youngsters. After a while even the most sympathetic teachers lost patience with him and came to believe that he wound people up. Sometimes John sat in my room and sobbed bitterly. He felt that people didn't care. From time to time his overly intellectual persona disappeared and he exploded into terrible rages. Despite his intelligence he felt at the mercy of events and of himself. His inability to talk about the future was striking. At home his mother told me he was always working at his computer. John was beginning to fit a pattern of behaviour and character we have come to know as Asperger Syndrome.

We set great store in analytic psychotherapy on *thinking* about our difficulties rather than *doing* things to avoid feeling or constructing meaning, yet the literature on the importance of language development in order to do this and its significance for the individual in terms of self-management and our ability to relate to others is sparse in psychotherapeutic theory. *Meaning* and the importance of meaning-making is often referred to without any reference to language at all. This is of course with the notable exception of the French psychoanalyst Jacques Lacan, who is often overlooked or derided by the Anglo-Saxon clinician for making too much fuss about language. This absence of reference to language seems to me to be particularly true in the way the Kleinian ideal of communication through projective identification is utilised. For instance, Anne Alvarez, a clinician famous for her work with autistic children and children with Asperger Syndrome, demonstrates in her book *Live Company* (1992) her understanding of Bion's application of this Kleinian notion. She defines projective identification as 'getting someone to do our thinking for us' (1992: 4). How is thinking to be done?

Bion suggested that some projective identifications expressed a need to communicate something to someone at a very profound level; he began to see this as related to a fundamental process in normal development and compared the analyst's containment and transformation of the patient's thoughts and feelings to the primitive but powerful pre-verbal communication which takes place between mothers and tiny infants. The mother's capacity for reverie, he wrote, could contain the infant's crises and excitements and transform them into bearable experiences.

Alvarez goes on to say that Bion suggested that this was a normal maternal function and that many clinicians have begun to consider this quality of understanding as central to their work with all patients, not only the psychiatrically ill (Bion [1962] 1984, 1965, quoted in Alvarez 1992: 4). The concept of *containment* becomes paramount, 'brave receptive listening to what the child feels was done to him' (Alvarez 1992: 5). Philosophically, in all this there is a suggestion that meaning can exist outside of linguistic practices, that there are mechanisms outside of language, mysteriously available to 'knowledge'. This is perhaps not what Bion intended, since alongside this was his notion of 'nameless dread' which for him conveyed the kind of anxiety he had perceived in very psychotic patients when they were unable to represent things in language. 'Nameless dread' is a primary anxiety in the infant and can happen to all of us throughout life when experience cannot be contained in language and meaning cannot be made.

The Lacanian child analyst Maud Mannoni (1987) places great emphasis on the importance of language in the development of the child. She disputes any notion of a pre-verbal stage of development or that the fate of the child rests on the quality of his nursing care. She writes:

> The child has a place in parental discourse before he is born, in that sense there is no 'pre-verbal stage.' The infant has a name; he will be 'spoken' so long as he is an object of care; the neglect of his needs to which we attach so much importance as in regard to frustrations will have far less effect on him than the accidents of discourse that surround him. The specifically human environment is neither biological nor social but linguistic.
>
> (Mannoni 1987: 217)

24

These may be difficult ideas for the Anglo-Saxon clinician who may not be comfortable using a linguistic metaphor to conceptualise what they consider to be an 'early' or 'pre-verbal' deficit. For instance, there is an interesting debate in contemporary psycho-analytic thinking as to the roots of autism, or failure to communicate. Culturally we are fascinated by this disorder and disorders of what we might think of as 'the autistic spectrum' like Asperger Syndrome. We read articles in the newspapers written by mothers who have one or sometimes more than one autistic child. We speculate whether these disorders are on the increase in our society or if they are simply better diagnosed at this time in history. We wonder what 'causes' autism, and what it might be which goes so wrong at the beginning of life and development. Is autism, for instance, the result of brain damage, or even a byproduct of a vaccination? Secretly and rather guiltily we might wonder if mothers 'cause' autism in their children. The link with a vaccine seems to have come about because many autistic disorders are diagnosed around the time at which a vaccine is administered. Studies in Denmark have suggested that this is why the causal link is so easily made; not that the vaccine 'causes' autism but rather that it is administered at the time in a child's development when autistic features are manifesting themselves. In fact, this is also the time in development when the child begins to speak. Failure to speak and to communicate becomes a basis for a diagnosis of autism. For the Lacanian analyst, autism is a disorder of language and as such is a psychotic illness presenting a very different mental structuring from a neurotic one.

In order for a clinician in the Anglo-Saxon tradition to begin to think about this disorder, she is likely to utilise metaphors of boundary and space, and rather than emphasise the linguistic environment of the mother and infant, would prioritise the earliest diffuse bodily experience between the two. Thinkers in this group would view a 'self' as emerging from consistent rhythmical experiences of sensory cohesion and boundedness between mother and infant. In this way the infant can feel safe inside a skin boundary rather than being infused with primitive terrors of leaking out of his sphincters into shapeless space. These metaphors of boundary and space are familiar to clinicians as part of the object relations tradition in the work of D. W. Winnicott. They are articulated with particular relevance to autism by the American psychoanalyst, Thomas Ogden (1992). Ogden conceives of the notion of a 'pre-symbolic' mode of experience he refers to as the 'autistic-contiguous position'. The metaphor he starts out with is a spatial one, one of 'shape'. The danger for the infant is that he will experience 'formless dread'. The terror is of losing shape, of the loss of boundary, of bodies dissolving and leaking or falling into space. Ogden prioritises the quality of sensory communication between mother and infant in order to bring about these feelings of safety. 'It is', says Ogden (1992: 52), 'a time of touching and cooing, of surfaces touching one another'. He echoes Francis Tustin, a well known writer on autism of the British object relations school, who believed in the healing power of interactions with the mother to prevent a too acute sense of separateness. If the sense of separateness, which is an inevitable experience even in earliest infancy, is too acute, then what comes about is 'an awareness of bodily experience which results in an agony of consciousness' (Tustin 1986: 46). It is this agony of consciousness which, in her view, the autistic child is trying to avoid.

What is craved is absolutely reliable comfort and protection. This is provided through the pathological use of devices described by Tustin as 'autistic shapes'. These are not always easy to conceptualise but would seem to be a way of clinging to sensory experience and communicating through manipulating hard or soft objects or bits of the body as a form of self-soothing, and as a substitute for relationships. For instance, Ogden (1992) describes a patient who paradoxically needed to smell bad in order to hold himself together and stay connected to others. Pathological autism aims at the absolute elimination of the unknown and the unpredictable. Safety becomes paramount. Ogden (1992: 60) states that for the autistic child, 'No person can compete with the capacity of never changing autistic shapes and objects to provide absolutely reliable comfort and protection'.

Thus, the autistic child shapes experience by utilising sensory-dominated ways of being, to gain absolute consistency and to insulate a potential self from people and relationships: rocking, watching the same video over and over again, repeating the same words and phrases, no brown or yellow food. For Ogden and Tustin, these are not just different ways of processing experience, but are powerful defences aimed at protecting the individual from 'unspeakable terror'. And they manifest a breakdown in the ability to attribute meaning to experience. In this way these analysts understand what is behind the compulsivity, repetition and desire for sameness of the autistic child.

Interestingly, Ogden moves in the same chapter from a spatial metaphor, 'formless dread', to a linguistic one, 'unspeakable terror', as though they were interchangeable. For thinkers like the British psychoanalyst Wilfred Bion, or the French psychoanalyst Jacques Lacan, these metaphors would not be the same at all and they would make careful distinctions between them. For instance, Ogden links these defensive manoeuvres to a breakdown in the ability to attribute meaning to experience without elaborating on this in any way. It is curious then to see that at the end of his chapter on 'the autistic contiguous position', having detailed the primary anxiety as one of bodily dissolution stemming from a too acute experience of separation anxiety, he shares with us as a deeply personal example of this kind of anxiety, a powerful experience of a word losing meaning for him:

> After dinner one night while I was sitting at the dining room table, it suddenly occurred to me how strange it was that the thing called a napkin was named by the conjunction of sounds 'nap' and 'kin'. I repeated the sound over and over again until I began to get the frightening feeling that these sounds had no connection at all to the thing I was looking at. I could not get these sounds to 'mean' the thing that they had meant only minutes before. The link was broken and to my horror could not be mended by an act of will. I imagined that I could, if I chose to, destroy the power of any and all words to 'mean' something if I thought about them one at a time in this way. At that point I had the very disturbing feeling I had discovered a way to drive myself crazy. I imagined that all things in the world would come to feel as disconnected as the napkin had become for me now that it had become disconnected from the word which formerly named it. Further I felt that I could become utterly disconnected from the rest of the world because all other people would still share in a 'natural', i.e. a still meaningful system of words. Such is the nature of the beginnings of a collapse of the dialectic of experience in the direction of sensation dominated experience that is unmediated by the use of symbols.
>
> (Ogden 1992: 80)

The terror becomes one of 'entrapment' in a world of sensation. Ogden seems almost unconsciously to have moved towards Bion's notion of 'nameless dread', a primary anxiety for the infant and for all of us throughout life when experience cannot be contained in language and meaning cannot be made. At the end of his chapter, 'skin' has become metaphorical for Ogden. It stands for the binding power of words and language. The dominant terror has become, for him, loss of meaning rather than separation.

Given our cultural fascination with autism, it is not surprising that two recently published books on this topic have won awards. One was written by Luke Jackson (2002) when he was 13 years old and is an account of what his life was like. Luke describes Asperger Syndrome as a 'communication disorder' and in his remarkable book is able to overcome the paradox of how to find language to describe such a condition, one some would describe as a disorder 'on the higher functioning end' of the autistic spectrum (Attwood 1998).

In writing his account, Luke Jackson does not attempt to offer any explanations or causes for his condition but, with remarkable fluency, he documents what it is like to *be* him, and what it is like to be part of his family, which consists of his three brothers and his three sisters. His two younger brothers suffer from attention deficit disorder and autism respectively. Luke begins by focusing on physical symptoms and sensory deficiencies within the family members. He describes his extended family as being 'immune sensitive'. His mother is acutely sensitive to certain smells and sounds, so she cannot bear the cinema, for instance. His aunt suffers from chronic asthma, hay fever and a multitude of allergy problems. All the children in the Jackson family suffer from these immune and allergy problems in varying degrees and Luke points out that this is a phenomenon of autistic families. They lack a stimulus barrier and the world bombards them with sensory stimulation. It is as though the family is particularly thin-skinned. In order to survive, the family have worked hard at desensitising themselves and building up an immunity to experiences the rest of us take for granted but which the family find hard to bear, such as the sound of school bells, the smell of animals at the zoo, the smell of paint or the texture of sand. Luke describes how he and other Asperger sufferers have developed strategies to protect themselves from being overwhelmed. These take the form of ritualistic behaviours and the kinds of compulsion which we have come to associate with autism. Luke carried pencils around with him for years. He could not be without them, perhaps demonstrating what Blos would have described as 'concretisation', or what Tustin may have considered 'an autistic shape'. It is interesting to me that pencils are things which have the potential for representation. Luke at that time was not confident in representing things, but he did carry the *potential* within him. Autistic shapes become not just substitutes for people but substitutes for representation itself. The adult who experiences autistic states will reveal how he holds himself together through speech acts and gestures as he begins to speak.

Understanding the quality of terror and anxiety from which Luke works so hard to protect himself is difficult. Once again we need to return to the topic of skin. One of Luke's soothing rituals was to gaze at lava lamps. Reading about Luke's fascination with lava lamps made me think of the work of the psychoanalyst Esther Bick (1985). She was an early pioneer in child development who wrote about the importance that skin contact has in early development in helping babies to overcome primitive life and death terrors. Like Tustin and Ogden she conceived of these terrors as experienced by infants as feeling like falling to bits or spilling over and out of their skin. She observed many babies in interaction with their mothers: babies who were not being held by their mothers or who were particularly frightened would focus on sensory stimuli like electric lights or the sound of the washing machine to soothe them. Bick describes such children as growing up intensely conservative and terrified of change. They would develop modes of compulsive behaviour which she describes as a 'second skin formation'. It would be interesting with hindsight to know about the language development of the children whom Bick observed. This second skin formation seems like a substitute for language or the capacity for verbalised thought as a way of dealing with anxiety or the overwhelming influx of experience. It is a way of remaining trapped in what Freud referred to as a 'body ego', without having made any of the transformations towards the binding power of language.

Luke's need for secondary skin formations of this kind reflects his difficulties with language. Concretisation seems most in evidence in him when it comes to speech and language: 'I have lost count of the number of times I have been told to copy a title off the blackboard and then sat patiently waiting to be told what to do next, whilst everyone scribbled frantically' (Jackson 2002: 114). Luke says that for the adolescent and teenage person with Asperger Syndrome, 'deciphering other kids' meanings is harder than deciphering ancient hieroglyphics' (2002: 100). He describes how 'logical people' seem to him: 'Non Asperger's Syndrome people say things they don't mean, miss out things they do mean, do all sorts of strange things with their faces which apparently change the meanings of their words – and they say Asperger's Syndrome people are odd' (2002: 108).

Luke particularly advises those communicating with Asperger sufferers not to use metaphors like 'beating around the bush' or 'a face like thunder' or to expect him to understand how other people feel. He comes across like Mr Spock, the character from the television space series, *Star Trek*, who was bewildered by emotion and emotional people and who approached the world in a literal and rational way. Luke behaves like an alien from Vulcan, which is what causes other people to react so violently towards sufferers like him and to treat them like 'freaks and geeks'. It is as though people with Asperger Syndrome and its related disorders have opted out from the irrationality of language, metaphor and emotion.

This opting out is of particular significance from the point of view of Lacan. What is being rejected is a developmental step he refers to as entering into 'the name of the father' (Lacan 1956). This is a complex moment of development and mental organisation. It embraces the deep structures of language to which we are all subject, as well as the existence of all that has been there before us. That includes the kinship structure into which we are born, the realisation that we possess a pre-history, the structure of our parents' union and the family constellations with which we must deal. In particular, in order to become a self or what Lacan would refer to as a *subject*, we must agree to accept and participate in the signifying material at our disposal – our language. This is a hugely important step in our development and follows Freud's belief that the acquisition of language was a great cultural achievement. According to Lacan, we need to use language in order to express meaning in a discourse designed to communicate and reconcile it with various received meanings (1956: 83). The autistic child markedly does *not* subject himself to 'commonly admitted discourse' and a child with Asperger Syndrome only partially does so. For thinkers like Ogden and Tustin, this would reveal a catastrophic breakdown in the earliest nursing encounters that enable an infant to achieve a secure sense of boundaried self, with a concept of inside and outside. For Lacanian thinkers however, the refusal of language equates to a refusal of all that the father stands for and leaves us tied to our mother. This is perhaps still best expressed by Freud himself when, in *Moses and Monotheism* he states:

This turning from the mother to the father points in addition to a victory of intellectuality over sensuality – that is, an advance in civilisation since maternity is proved by the evidence of the senses while paternity is a hypothesis based on an inference and a premise. Taking sides in this way with a thought process in preference to a sense perception has proved to be a momentous step.

(Freud 1939: 114)

The implications of this are explored in fictional form in the second prize-winning book on the topic of autistic disorder: the novel *The Curious Incident of the Dog in the Night-time* by Mark Haddon (2003). Christopher, the narrator, aged 15 and a sufferer from Asperger Syndrome or some unnamed high functioning autistic disorder, struggles both with language and with his fear of his father. At times the two seem linked. Christopher possesses a highly sophisticated mathematical intelligence. He will take his maths A level examination at the age of 15 and will probably get a grade A. He understands prime numbers, he has a photographic memory and he can understand and demonstrate the Monty Hall problem – a maths problem which has defeated many of the world's mathematical experts. He sees through the stereotypical view of his teacher that his love of maths has anything to do with 'safety':

Mr Jeavons said that I liked maths because it was safe. He said I liked maths because it meant solving problems, and these were difficult and interesting but there was always a straightforward answer at the end. And what he meant was that maths wasn't like that because in life there are no straightforward answers at the end. I know he meant this because this is what he said. This is because Mr Jeavons doesn't understand numbers . . . numbers are sometimes very complicated and not very straightforward at all.

(Haddon 2003: 82)

Christopher is mystified by language however. He likes things to be 'real' and he is afraid of lies. He sees metaphor as lies. Here he shows us his struggle with the notion of being the 'apple of someone's eye': 'When I try to make a picture of the phrase in my head it just confuses me because imagining an apple in someone's eye doesn't have anything to do with liking someone a lot and makes you forget what the person was talking about' (2003: 20).

At one point in the novel Christopher tells us that his name is a metaphor. His mother has explained to him that it was the name given to St Christopher because he carried Jesus Christ across a river: 'Mother used to say that it meant Christopher was a nice name because it was a story about someone being kind and helpful but I don't want my name to be about being kind and helpful. I want my name to mean me' (2000: 20).

Christopher seems to be caught up in a fear that he will have to be someone for someone else. He fears that his identity is fixed and that words are fixed. Rather than feeling he has been named in relation to another, his fear is that he has been *included in* the Other and caught up in their desires. According to Mannoni (1987), the psychotic child and the mother often form a single body: 'The child tries to pour himself into the mould of the other's desire, from conception, playing a role for the mother on the phantasy plane' (p. 96). He becomes an object without desires of his own whose sole purpose is to is to fill the maternal void, what Mannoni calls the mother's 'lack in being'. The child's object is to be the mother's phantasy object – what Lacan termed 'the phallus'. The child is attempting to protect the parents against the unmask-ing of the very heart of their neurosis (Mannoni 1987: 168.) As a result, his body is inhabited by panic and 'he lacks the symbolic dimension that would enable him to confront the desire of the other without being ensnared by him' (1993: 168).

Without language and speech, Christopher is prone to experi-ences of sensory overload and seemingly irrational rages – going shopping in a crowded arcade with his mother makes him lie on the floor and scream. He cannot eat brown or yellow food. He is acutely sensitive to smell: 'My memory has a smelltrack which is like a sound track'. He cannot bear to be touched, not even by his parents, and will allow them only to touch the palm of his hands. Christopher seems fiercely protective of his skin boundary, his bodily self. In many ways he lives in a constant state of fear and vigilance, using superstition and compulsive ritual to feel safe – five red cars in a row means a Super Good Day and he can venture out; five yellow cars might mean he has to stay at home. He is speechless with terror.

Haddon's novel is a powerful metaphor of the compromise we must make in being subjected to language. Lacan described us as being 'afflicted by language'. We know, as Luke and Christopher know, that language is an unreliable and idiosyncratic mode of correspondence but it is all that we have. Christopher finds in his thoughtful female teacher someone who can reconcile him to language and help him give an account of himself. As therapists we too spend some time reconciling patients to speech rather than action. What's the point of just talking about things? I want to get on and do things, they say. Christopher masters his fear and rage at his father in the act of writing and telling his story. He demonstrates what Freud said: that the struggle to contain our feelings in thought, the act of sublimation, is an epic struggle, an Oedipal struggle. Coming to terms with language is an epic struggle, like coming to terms with the lies and violence at the heart of family life. When Christopher's mother leaves the family to go off with the man next door, Christopher is told that she is dead. In a fit of frustration, his father kills the dog next door, and then lies about doing so. Christopher's distrust of his father' language as a meaning-making vehicle has become intelligible. Through writing a novel, through giving an account of himself in language rather than through impulsive action like his father, he transcends him and becomes potent. It is this potency through mastery that telling a story can bring: 'I will get a first class honours degree and I will become a scientist. And I know I can do this because I went to London and because I solved the mystery of who killed Wellington and I found my mother and I was brave and I wrote a book and that means I can do anything' (Haddon 2003: 268).

Christopher speaks in the first person for Mark Haddon, reminding us of the alienation of the subject from himself and returning us to the initial question: who is speaking here and to whom?

Luke Jackson has made similar transformations through the process of writing his book. In his chapter on school and bullying he shows how his teachers seemed ignorant of his condition and his need for clear instructions. He comments that he would be pounced on later as 'unfortunate prey'. I was impressed that having spent much of his book explaining his difficulties with metaphor he was able to convey the violence he experienced in these actions and his feelings of animal helplessness. Through the use of metaphor, he is able to tell us 'what it is like' and transforms the experience from a passive one into an experience of active mastery. This ability to describe what it is like, to represent these complex feeling states in language is what Lacan (1955) would describe as 'full speech' in the terms of the quotation at the beginning of this chapter. At the end of his book, through the act of writing, Luke has overcome much of his 'communication disorder' which is something we hope for in our patients in psychotherapy and is what gives them hope in turn. It is interesting to me that Luke subtitles his book *A User's Guide to Adolescence*. It is as though he realises, through the act of writing, that his dilemma of finding the right words is a crisis universal to all adolescents and to adults in the adolescent state, not just those who suffer from Asperger Syndrome.

3

DIAGNOSIS: SHOULD WE
EVEN BEGIN?

In assessing referrals for psychotherapy or psychoanalysis
it is best to avoid the term *diagnosis* because it becomes
confused with psychiatric diagnosis and the medical
treatment of patients.

(Hinshelwood 1991: 166)

Robert Hinshelwood asserts that the analytic practitioner must not
behave or speak as though psychoanalysis or psychotherapy were
equivalent to medical treatment, even though envy or ambition
might lead some of us onto such paths. A physical condition can be
recognised through tests. It can then be treated in various ways in
which best practice and often (but not always) statistics lead us
to believe that improvement will follow. In psychotherapy, the
research base is not comparable. Very few factors have been iso-
lated and identified, and those that we have are very general. For
example, empathy, genuineness and respect, the core conditions
advocated by Carl Rogers (1965), have been shown to affect
outcome as reported by counselling patients. As far as I am aware
at the time of writing, no study has shown a clear advantage of any
one model of psychotherapy over any other. Therefore the factors
that are likely to emerge as helpful to patients will be likely to
extend across models and be fairly general.

There is a debate to be held over the issue of diagnosis, its use
and its dangers for the clinician. Since R. D. Laing in the 1960s
and Thomas Szasz in 1972 ([1972] 1984) we have no excuse to
insert ourselves in the power structure of diagnostic categories if we
are going to use them as straitjackets. The act of diagnosis prob-
lematises the patient. What emerges is a relationship to a problem

which interests the clinician and entitles the patient to his therapy. Diagnosis gives permission for regression. If I am ill, I need to be looked after. The process of assessment with or without diagnosis is therefore a stage in the development of the therapeutic state and it leads back to the earliest state that is still present in the patient. On the other hand, the clinician must take due care of the patient. Care implies a responsible assessment of the pathology being brought and its probable response to the particular method of treatment to be used. New approaches have to emerge for the new patient, even though the psychoanalytic perspective is usually favourably inclined to descriptive categories such as making a distinction between the neurotic structure and the perverse or psychotic. Above all, I shall be looking at the stage of evolution of the narrative self that is shown to me. The patient's use of language, both verbal and behavioural, will be my primary concern.

Jeremy Holmes (1995) claims to belong to the 'grand opera' school of assessment. His models were Heinz Wolff and Henry Rey at the Maudsley Hospital Psychotherapy Department. He describes Wolff as the charismatic assessor to whom the patient felt he could tell anything. This was aided by the fact that he appeared to fall asleep, allowing the patient to expand on the most difficult areas of his story in peace. Holmes comments ironically that the patients left the assessment bathed in cathartic tears, but 'he promises the earth – and leaves it to the Registrar to deliver it' (p. 27). Any clinician faced with the pain of a patient who is newly recognising whatever his problem is will want to promise the earth. For some of them, realism will lead to a wish to retreat, without promising anything. For others, the temptation may well be to hold out some hope, even if better judgement might indicate that there is actually very little hope of improvement in that particular case. Few clinicians have the option of handing the case over to a registrar as Wolff did. However, some may well be assessing for an agency so that the person seeing the patient will not be the person doing the assessment. That is a situation in which additional skills of a different sort are required.

The prospective patient who meets an assessor in an agency usually finds that she is an experienced and wise therapist who is very good at facilitating self-revelation and is very well able to respond in a way that is helpful. All the precepts about giving an appropriate trial interpretation are likely to be second nature to this clinician. Then, the patient is faced with the painful situation that this ideal and new-found parent tells him that the new relationship will last for only one session. The person who will see him in the longer term will be someone different.

The degree of distress can also be diagnostic. A prospective patient might be overwhelmed by the thought of having a different clinician from the one who conducted the assessment. He would be likely to have difficulty with the deprivations of short- or long-term psychoanalytic psychotherapy. Such people often self-select by opting out of further sessions. If, on the other hand, they do continue to seek psychotherapy, the agency has a difficult problem in deciding on its degree of responsibility for the treatment. Most agencies will undoubtedly seek to make an appropriate referral, perhaps to a place that offers supportive counselling or specialised help.

When the parameters of the assessment session itself have been made clear, there are general principles that most psychoanalytic practitioners would be likely to have in mind.

Freud was interested in whether there were two or three persons in a relationship, whether in reality or in mind. Following Freud's line of thought, we can define one parameter of a relationship as the number of people or images of people in it. For the analytic therapist this will amount to an Oedipal problem or a pre-Oedipal problem. The latter is likely to require longer-term work and to involve strong attachment to the therapist. The former might be an indication for time-limited therapy of a year or less.

Patients whose difficulties relate to the earliest stages of development will show the defences that a Kleinian would describe as most primitive: we might identify splitting, excessive projection or paranoia. These will make for more difficult analytic conditions because these defences make it more difficult to form a relationship with the clinician in which the neurosis can be redeveloped and embellished until the fulcrum of the analytic work can begin to bear on it. Nevertheless, as Freud (1905) recognised, we often work with patients who 'are permanently unfit for existence'. Yet even those who are severely narcissistic can show themselves to be capable of analytic work. The conclusion that most contemporary clinicians have reached is that the pathology may be less a determinant than the motivation and degree of willingness that the patient displays to allow the illness to be apparent to the practitioner and to be addressed by her.

The *Diagnostic and Statistical Manual* (*DSM*) provides a description of the recognised conditions and syndromes where there is sufficient to enable a practitioner to assign a patient to a category.

In trainee essays on the pathology of patients to be seen in a counselling service, I have come across statements such as: 'the patient is showing signs of bipolar disorder and, according to *DSM IV* (American Psychiatric Association 2000), should be diagnosed as manic depressive'. This kind of diagnosis is very understandable in that trainees are naturally anxious about the degree of uncertainty and waiting that is asked of them in the process of psychodynamic work. They are eager for any kind of certainty and are likely to seize on anything that seems to offer it. Clearly a *DSM IV* diagnosis on its own will not lead to any further understanding of the individual. Its most useful place will be in coming to a decision about the patients who will *not* be helped by psychodynamic probing and uncovering. No analytic practitioner would deliver any such diagnosis in their analytic capacity and would probably have to work hard with a patient who had been given such a diagnosis by a psychiatrist.

Take for example the patient who had been told in a psychiatric service that he has a borderline personality disorder.

He was at first shocked and then, in some hidden part of himself, pleased. He found his way to an analytic clinician. The work for some time consisted in dealing with the patient's confident statement that there was nothing he could do about his furious rages or his failure to preserve relationships. All was caused by his personality disorder. Why then had he come to see a clinician? One hypothesis would be that he had come to receive confirmation that nothing he could do would rid him of his original sin. If he were marked out as particularly unfit for relationships, then so be it and let others beware. The only plan that he could contemplate was that his clinician would find some way of changing him without any effort on his part.

The clinician in this situation is dealing with either a moral or a philosophical problem. Why would the patient ever be motivated to care about becoming more desirable? Does he hate humanity so much that he has no wish to play his part with others as a human being? Does he feel that he is capable of playing a part in a relationship so that he is loved by another? Some of the philosophical thinking of the twentieth century has been about these questions of responsibility. Emanuel Levinas (1996) saw responsibility for the Other as the defining quality of human morality.

When we encounter another we have to greet him. We can do so either as one being to another or as one being to a thing. This view interrogates the difference that Martin Buber ([1923] 1958) established (Rowan 2001). What happens when a clinician greets a patient as another being, equal but different from herself and how is that different from greeting him as a thing? The answer is to be found only in the clinician's emotional response to the patient.

Fear is one of the emotions in the clinician that can lead to defending against meeting the person in the first encounter at the level of existence as two human beings capable of moving and being moved in all sorts of ways:

> Mr T. asks for therapy from a clinician who has been recommended to him by a colleague. He begins by looking seductively at the woman clinician and says, 'You look like someone who could understand a man's problems.' Mrs S., the clinician, is at once on the defensive. She notes the seductive tone and expression with which this is said and, because she can see that the man is attractive, she recognises that he will try to make a sexual conquest. She removes herself from the arena in her own mind, because there is a possibility that otherwise she might respond to him. She thinks to herself: this man is a seducer. He avoids his own powerlessness by seeking to exert power over the people he encounters.

This may well be a correct and useful formulation but it is not sufficient. It leaves out the necessary humanity of the contact. To carry out a full meeting, the clinician might think: this is an attractive man; I am a woman and somehow we have to make something of this encounter without allowing it to be sexual. The solution is not to deny the potential but to make use of it.

Ready diagnosis puts another person into the category of 'a manic depressive' or 'a hysteric'. These categories may help us to think about areas of disturbance and possible technique that could be helpful and if they are in the mind of the clinician they may be used appropriately at the beginning. On the other hand, they may reify the illness so that the person becomes invisible. We all need some sort of safety, particularly in the dangerous work that we do. One form of self-preservation might be to differentiate the patient from the clinician as not only the sick one but the sickness itself.

The clinician can nevertheless bear in mind the need for a

39

diagnosis of any mental illness that might be a contra-indication for psychotherapy given her own competence and experience. She will also be aware of the need of the person before her for some immediate help. She may wish to consider other aspects of suitability before agreeing to begin ongoing work. In Holmes' view, motivation is the main factor to consider along with the severity of the pathology. Thus, for example, moderate narcissism might not prevent the possibility of a useful analysis but severe narcissism might make it too difficult for the patient to submit himself to the demands and deprivations of therapy. Holmes uses the aphorism that the patient must be 'sick enough to need it, but healthy enough to stand it' (Holmes 1995: 39). Seeking evidence of being healthy enough, he is aware that some of our most difficult patients are unlikely to have good relationships in any area of their lives so the existence of a partner or a 'good enough' work experience would be encouraging.

Those who have moved beyond this early stage will be the people whose difficulties arise in the Oedipal stage and are bothered by the demands and deprivations of the triangular relationship that exists when the third person disrupts the infantile duo. Such patients will be using repression and one of the therapist's tasks will be to help in the safe recovery of the repressed dangerous desires. The patient will not be able to allow this recovery until he can separate internal injunctions that relate to parental figures of the past from those that relate to partners (and of course the clinician) in the present.

This is the Freudian point of view and since his most productive period in the first third of the twentieth century, many others have developed theoretical structures based on his pioneering ideas. A 'relational model', the work of Safran and Muran (2000), challenges the conflict model of Freud in which the patient's desires to be accepted and loved conflict with the permission that society may or may not give for action based on desire. Safran and Muran, like the object relations school, emphasise the need to steer a path between nihilism and naive realism. Their solution is a form of constructivism: 'Thus although there is no ideal reality independent of the perceiver, reality is more than simply a reflection of the perceiver's mind. In a sense then, truth is both constructed and discovered' (2000: 35). An aspect of this approach is that the clinician needs to maintain a position which Safran and Muran delineate as remaining a 'beginner'. Experts by definition know what is needed and what they must do. The patient will often push the practitioner to accept expert status, but an open mind is the only attitude that is suited to the practice of psychotherapy. Paradoxically, this does not mean that the clinician need abrogate her expertise. She undoubtedly has expertise but it is in such unique areas as maintaining neutrality and agnosticism. This attitude is entirely consistent with an egalitarian view of psychotherapy. The clinician has to take on responsibility for some areas of the work and the patient is inevitably responsible for his own conduct and his own use of the experience. Together in the first session they piece together something that both can recognise as an adequate statement of a truth.

The assessing clinician has an immensely difficult job and could not do it without considerable expertise. The best guides to the kind of expertise needed are probably the latest version of the *DSM* and a study such as *What Works for Whom?* by Fonagy (2000). Even those two works together will offer guidance on only typical and fairly gross symptomatology. Sometimes, if there is mental illness, a well trained practitioner can have little doubt about the nature of the problem or the need for an appropriate and well contained setting.

On the other hand, what are we to think about Mr J. who presents with a difficulty in his work relationship but turns out to have lost his father to cancer two years before? He is apparently schizoid and shows little sign of being able to make an affective relationship. The clinician must choose between on the one hand a brief contract, perhaps using cognitive techniques to help Mr J. to arrive at a better solution to his problems at work, and on the other the long-term option which will take at least 24 sessions (and probably longer), exploring the death of his father and the anxiety that his ambivalent feelings for his father has created in his relationships with men who remind him of his father. Experience will tell us that it is possible to work with loss and bereavement in the fairly short term, following such models as that of Elisabeth Kubler Ross (1973). These writers have taken a developmental view of bereavement and would probably believe that the bereavement counsellor's job is to find out where the process has reached a sticking point and why it is not continuing to evolve.

An analytic clinician looking at the same problem will be likely to work with it at a level that transfers some of the effects of the relationship with the lost person to the clinician so that the most powerful emotions of love, anger, hate and sadness can be experienced in the present, not just recollected. Embarking on this kind of work is not responsible or ethical if it is known that there will be

41

very limited time. A patient needs many sessions in which to allow such emotions to surface in relation to the clinician and many more in which to express them before he will be ready to move on. A premature ending will simply add to the bereavement and will mean that more symptoms will arise until and unless a clinician can be found who will be able to work through the experience patiently, letting it take as long as it takes. In our present state of knowledge, the length of time needed cannot be predicted with certainty.

In most cases, we would wish to have the option of open-ended work if we are embarking on anything of this sort. Extended assessment may help where there is doubt about the suitability of the model for the patient. Donald Winnicott (1988) wrote of the *theoretical first session*, meaning that the first session functions may need to be spread over many actual sessions in time. We have a few stars to guide us, but on the whole the strength of feeling with which anyone will enter into the therapeutic arena is variable and not well related to the nature of the behaviour shown. The clinician must therefore rely on clinical experience and theoretical orientation to reach a decision about the possible length of a contract. In most cases there will also be a supervisor involved who will have his or her own agenda. Some supervisors are not experienced in time-limited work but are appointed to supervise counsellors in general practice just because they are well respected clinicians. Such practitioners will have much to offer but may not recognise the complexity of the problem that counsellors face when the choice of length of contract is left to them.

If a counsellor expresses the conviction that a given patient *needs* to be seen for more than 6 or 12 sessions, the supervisor is unlikely to disagree. She must, however, try to help the counsellor to make decisions that are based on more than mere liking. A profound and unshifting dislike of the patient might be a contra-indication, but liking is certainly not an indication for psychoanalytic psychotherapy or psychodynamic counselling. If either reaction is strongly marked, of course, the clinician will be well advised to consider her own involvement in the relationship and what the patient represents for her. Sometimes, a patient is impossible to like. That may not be a matter of the chemistry between him and the clinician but may be an important indication of the nature of the difficulty.

A prospective patient, Ms C., arrives in the consulting room, looks round and begins: 'I expected something different from this. This is much too comfortable. Almost suburban don't you think? Perhaps you wanted it to have that effect. Did you? Are you the kind of person who doesn't have any sense of style at all?'

This patient irritated me strongly in the first session. I take notice of my irritation and her inability to allow any kind of mutual respect to develop between us. I am made into a worthless and inferior object before I have said more than 'Good morning, come in'. Such an attitude must lead her into very difficult and unpleasant relationships so I can feel some sympathy for the person even before I have any idea of what the underlying aetiology might be. My ability to feel how unpleasant it must be to be her is important because without it my irritation would triumph and I would not wish to see her again. As it is, my professional self is curious to know what can drive someone to such a degree of apparent envy and to such counterproductive relating. I note the envy and competitiveness and also am interested to know with whom she is competing. I am aware too, that she is posing questions to both of us about what she can expect from this rather worthless and probably easily defeated clinician. The reality of course is that I am not yet defeated but I have no special need to demonstrate that to her in any other way than by simply carrying on doing my job as best I can.

Holmes (1995: 33) points out that he is looking for three things, of which the ability to create a good rapport is one, but only one:

- the ability to form a good rapport or working alliance;
- the ability to work with interpretations; and
- the capacity to respond affectively within the session – to allow feelings of fear, anger or sadness to surface.

In Chapter 7 I will consider in more detail the nature and meaning of the term *working alliance*. It may perhaps for now be useful to consider that an ability to feel something positive for a patient who is behaving obnoxiously may be a necessary indication for the possibility of successful therapy. In my own view, the quality that I have to be able to find in myself for a prospective patient is

43

something like admiration or at least respect. I have to be able to feel that in spite of the difficulties that the patient is describing and his counterproductive response to them, this is a human being who has potential and who can already show some of the human qualities of endurance, or humour, or at least inventive symptoms and responses to his problems.

There is some research which can help us to think about the importance of consonance between clinician and patient. For example, Tracey (1988) studied 33 patients and the counsellors who worked with them at a university counselling service. The study found that at the beginning, patients felt themselves to be more responsible for their problems and for solving them than did their clinicians. The satisfaction with the first session was to some extent related to the degree of agreement that the patient was able to believe he could experience with his clinician. Dropout was also lower if the level of agreement was higher. Of course, many counsellors would take the analysis of a harsh superego to be the remit for the therapy and would no doubt disagree with a patient who thought that he was responsible for his own problems. This research bears out the importance of the listening process in which the clinician, at the beginning and *at least* during the assessment, is willing to listen to the patient's view of himself and not rush to superimpose her own.

Another view of the assessment process which is similarly based on quantitative evidence takes a view from sociology. Dreher (2002: 18) discusses the aims of psychoanalysis from the point of view of the potential researcher. She groups these aims into three areas:

- those from the theory and practice of psychoanalysis itself;
- those from the individual and social environments of the two persons involved;
- those from the sociocultural situation – the *Zeitgeist*.

The *Zeitgeist* includes all sorts of pressures and demands to be assessed by each individual in so far as any of them can actually be seen and consciously understood. Dreher suggests that she is talking of the flexible character that is required by modern capitalism. Presenting problems focus on the same core difficulties as they have for the last hundred years – isolation, loneliness, fear of death, the impossibility of communication, the frustration of powerlessness – but they are encased in new forms: the insecurity of all paid employment, the uncertainty of gender identity and the fragility of the relationships that once were bound by iron bands.

Some presenting problems are commonplace in twenty-first century western society. Ongoing research at *wpf Counselling and Psychotherapy* is showing that the most common presenting problem in an adult counselling service is depression. All sorts of reasons may be adduced to explain why so many feel lost and lacking in a self-image that is acceptable. The sense of a narrative self discussed in Chapter 2 gives coherence and meaning to a life. With lack of development of this aspect of the self, the individual has no belief in what Winnicott (1935) calls 'going on being'. The loss of religion may also be a contributing factor. Jung suggests that one of the main tasks of therapy is re-finding the religion of one's childhood. The loss of a coherent social system in which the individual is recognised and has a place may well be another. Cults and sects that provide a sense of belonging are successful because they help to mask the losses that the individual needs to acknowledge and mourn.

The second large area of defence against loss that we encounter in presenting problems is classified by psychoanalytic theory as the *manic defences*. These are described by Klein (1940) and Winnicott (1935) as defences against the recognition of loss, and its consequent depression. The defences themselves are very popular and most of us will recognise our own behaviour in the sort of mania described by Winnicott. Defences are useful and in fact are necessary for normal functioning. No one would regard the woman who tries to arrange a perfect Christmas for her family as mentally ill and yet such an effort may cause great strain and even lead to illness. Looking at the behaviour as a solution to the problem of avoiding the recognition of some loss or emptiness in her life might help such a woman to be less of a problem to herself and to her family. This is another situation in which time will be needed. If a clinician can help a patient to recognise the loss underlying a manic defence, the patient will be faced with the emptiness and the feared pain. Sessions will then be needed to help the patient to endure the rawness of the recognition until some other less damaging forms of defence can be discovered.

Each generation has its ways of describing mental unease. For the beginning of the twenty-first century, the most popular and evocative words for mental distress are *anxiety*, *stress* and *isolation*. Someone suffering from stress would in earlier times have been diagnosed as suffering from overwork or as 'highly strung'. This does not in itself tell us what the matter is or what is likely to emerge during the therapy. It does tell us that there is a failure in the defences. Freud's psychopathology can describe the situation well: the ego has not managed to defend itself against the demands of the superego or the id. Reason and the individual's ability to speak to himself have not been equal to the tasks set by some inner voice that demands more than the individual can achieve. This crisis will usually be presented in terms that sound as if the demands are coming from outside, and of course to some extent they are. The external demands will not cause stress, however, unless they are backed up by the internal structures which assent to them.

Clinicians are probably well aware of the current pressures generated in the UK by the *Patient's Charter*. In a culture of rights rather than responsibilities, the clinician is inevitably aware of the nature of the patient's demands and some of the limits of the extent to which they can be met in the therapy that she will be able to offer. 'Demand' is narcissistic and springs from the certainty of a baby that the world *is* himself. The recognition that others are independent and may not fit in to one's own image is both necessary and frightening, and if the parent did not help the child to reach that knowledge, the clinician will have to help the adult.

Defensive practice is a danger that emerges in a litigious society. The clinician will be less inclined to take risks by agreeing to see a patient who might be very difficult or who might not respond to conventional methods of treatment. In fact, all psychotherapy is a response to patients who do not get better if you prescribe two paracetamol. The pain is not easily removed in most cases and the clinician is always taking a risk, however straightforward the diagnosis might seem to be. Nevertheless, cautious diagnosis into broad areas of disturbance might help to distinguish those for whom treatment may be foolhardy or downright dangerous. All clinicians need to be able to see where there might be a risk of physical illness such as brain tumour or neurological disease and should be ready to refer for medical diagnosis whenever there is any question of a physiological problem that has not been excluded.

Most clinicians would be likely to agree, if pressed, that in the first session they are making some judgements about the prospective patient. One such judgement that is often made is that the patient must not be psychotic. Not all clinicians would regard psychosis as a contra-indication. Some would regard a blanket prohibition as unnecessary discrimination. The Philadelphia Association has been in the forefront of a movement to offer talking therapy to patients suffering from psychosis. There is still tension between the medical model of psychiatry and those clinicians who would wish to hand over all the treatment of this area to the doctors who control the pharmacological armoury. A blanket resolution *not* to treat such patients would amount to discrimination, but the most important question to ask is whether in such a case discrimination is of *benefit* to the patient. Treating someone who will suffer more as a result is probably a worse prospect than not treating someone out of misplaced caution.

Clinicians are perhaps a little less likely to overestimate their effectiveness through 'magical thinking' than other sectors of the population but they cannot rule it out:

> Frequently those who are in contact with psychiatric literature show two contradictory attitudes. On one hand, excitement or perhaps apprehension about the large number of discoveries using basic medical scientific technique . . . that have enriched psychiatric knowledge based on the medical model. But on the other hand, the fear that these findings are over valued and that uncritical acceptance may diminish the attention paid to psychological and socio-cultural factors in the appearance, manifestation and evolution of mental suffering.
>
> (Guimon 2001: 3)

The clinician may also be suffering from traces of the *palaeopsychiatry* referred to by Guimon (2001: 9) as 'the magical conception of mental illness' which prevails in the shamanist approach to medicine. Guimon also points out that the psychodynamic approach to mental suffering is seen by the clinicians themselves as having much in common with the shamans – for example, the interpretation of dreams as an essential part of the treatment.

The political implications of labelling mental illness in psychiatry is the thesis of Szasz's ([1972] 1984) attack on mythology. Labelling the most difficult and problematic sufferers as mentally ill may lead to throwing them into asylums. The more extreme forms of abuse may be less common than when Szasz was writing but there is still a risk that the psychotherapy profession as a whole and individuals in particular will set up criteria that become the boundary line beyond which we will never give an opportunity for talking treatment. Szasz was particularly concerned with hysteria and the way in which traditional psychiatry dealt with sufferers, dividing them into groups either as genuine sufferers or as malingerers, but consigning both to the category of 'mental illness'. Mental illness, he pointed out (p. 85), is not the antonym of malingering. He also pointed out that the term 'mental illness' might be used to evade a confrontation with the social, political and internal conflicts that form its structure and its content.

If we apply to assessment the ideas that Szasz and others have put forward, we might have to view the assessment process as designed to establish which patients can be helped by a specific clinician using a particular model. If language is privileged in the evolution of particular symptoms, then of course the process of assessment must be a matter of attempting to track the way in which the symptoms are concealing the words not spoken.

The reason for some degree of differential diagnosis in such a case is that the psychoanalytic clinician recognises the power of the instrument in her hands and will not add to the disturbance of a person whose grip on sanity is already very tenuous. We need to know what contra-indications there are and to use techniques that will uncover them.

Why might therapy increase disturbance? There are some obvious ways in which clinicians can increase the internal conflict and thence the anxiety that indicates its presence. We need to convey to a potential patient the sort of work that we will be offering them. Trial interpretations must be given carefully in the assessment interview. An interpretation about the patient's relationship to the therapist's breast is unwise in any terms but is also dangerous for the patient whose own sanity is fragile. He may fear that his therapist is madder than he is, and despair. Many people are going to find that sort of interpretation shocking. It might be taken as a metaphorical structure or a literal truth; in either case, a patient must be able to withstand the psychic shock of such an interpretation if that is the therapist's style, and not only that, but also be able to make use of it.

Why is an interpretation like this one such a shock? I have used the example with groups of trainees and they invariably gasp in amazement, particularly at the idea that such an interpretation might be made by a woman to a man in the first encounter. It brings up the issue of the erotic element in the relationship (see also Chapter 6). Any comment about the body of either the clinician or the patient is likely to bring out awareness of the two bodies in the room and the possibilities of how they will relate to each other. The therapist needs to feel safe enough with the patient to be able to work, but the patient needs to be able to be potent enough to become a danger to his woman therapist at some point. Other contra-indications can be seen in the response to the initial experience of the psychotherapy itself. Each practitioner has to find ways of recognising those people who are unlikely to benefit from a talking therapy and, more specifically, those people who will not benefit from that practitioner's own version of the model. Assessment will then have to look at the extent to which the person is likely to be able to make the symbolic leaps required for using transference by transferring the image back to one's original thought. A clinician may say to the person who comes into the consulting room with a cardboard cup and a straw, 'You are rejecting the good food that I might offer you for a McDonald's milkshake.' The new patient will be startled by this symbolic equation and may find it wholly ridiculous or inappropriate. On the other hand, he may be able to see that there is some sort of metaphorical justice in the idea. The person who is at least willing to consider the question and be interested rather than horrified at the idea that more is going on than is in his conscious awareness will be showing in some ways that he is a possible candidate for psychoanalytic work.

Negative assessments that psychoanalytic psychotherapy may be harmful to a given individual must be made. Hippocrates' first principle for medical practitioners is *not to do harm*. By any ethical or moral standards, the clinician is enjoined to make the same priority. Positive assessments must also be made. What will be helpful to this person is an important question to ask and each clinician must have her own schemas for making a psychodynamic formulation. A Kleinian clinician will be looking at the ways in which the prospective patient can be understood in terms of infantile unconscious phantasy and will regard the transference interpretation of this as the main therapeutic tool at her disposal.

An interesting task which has not yet been completed, as far as I know, might be to compare and contrast ways in which presenting problems can be formulated in terms of the different models of psychoanalytic therapy. Gedo and Goldberg (1975) attempted to look at development in individuals in terms of the development of psychoanalytic theory. Problems can certainly be formulated in terms of early dyadic relating or in terms of the problems of the triangulation that comes later. Using this knowledge may help the clinician to shape interpretations that meet the patient's level of feeling. Any thorough therapy will have to deal with both areas at some point.

Arnold Lazarus (1989) hypothesised a multimodal form of assessment which would not be in terms of the traditional pathologies developed by the Freudian therapies but would map developmental processes. John Rowan's *Ordinary Ecstasy* (2001) emphasises the holistic approach of humanistic psychology as opposed to reductionism, and this will have implications for the mapping that the clinician will be attempting. On the other hand, setting up the I-thou dialectic of the humanistic clinician is not necessarily in opposition to the free-floating attention of the analyst.

Discovering who might be helped and who might be harmed requires a matching of the theoretical orientation of the clinician with the capacity and desire of the patient. Presenting problems will be likely to group themselves in terms of what is offered by the main schools of psychoanalytic theory and clinical practice. For example, which patient could be usefully referred to an ego psychologist? As a graduate of a pluralistic training, I am well aware that for myself, patients show me in some cases a clear need for a particular theoretician's ideas or clinical approach. The guide for this is not quantitative, but qualitative. Each patient shows a predominant way of thinking and functioning and the assessment interview will give me the opportunity to come to the realisation that I am already thinking in broadly Freudian, Kleinian or Jungian terms about the way in which this person might be approached.

For example, a patient who speaks about a dream in the first session without being directly asked by me might be someone who has previous experience of therapy and knows what clinicians like, or might be someone whose dream life is powerful and already has an influence on their conscious life. This latter person will need me to allow fantasies to take shape, unfold and become numinous symbols. On the other hand, one person who came to see me told me immediately about a recurrent nightmare in which she saw a dead baby floating in a swimming pool. I noted the power of the imagery of the dream but my main interest was held by the way in which death was found in the unconscious depths where normally one can swim and survive. I could have taken this at a Jungian level, but I was also very much interested in the questions about life and sexuality that are raised by a dream about death. Freud would lead me to think about the symbolic equation: baby = penis =

faeces. I would think about what sexual questions this person might need to raise once we had understood why the potent image of the baby is represented as limp, drowned and helpless.

This dream brings me to think about the importance of the manifest content of the assessment session as well as its latent content. The patient mentioned above was in great psychological pain because she thought the dream was about a wish to kill her baby. I had of course to pay attention to the Freudian view of the dream in which some sort of wish or desire is making itself known. Perhaps she did want to kill her baby. Most mothers do at some point and it is often the repression of this wish and the attendant guilt and anxiety that causes damage, certainly to the mother and possibly to the baby also. If the ambivalence can be acknowledged, the conscious mind can work to deal with the negative feelings and the clinician can help the patient to accept that having such feelings is not in itself wicked, just the natural reaction of a woman whose life is no longer her own and will never be again. As one might expect there were also experiences in this person's history that led to her being unable to tolerate the helplessness and innocence of her baby. She had been abused by a woman in her adolescent years who had demanded sexual caresses from her and her own tenderness for her baby was unbearably mixed up with feelings of hate and fantasies of destruction.

No automatic formulation could have dealt with all the possibilities of this patient and her needs. What she gave me was merely an indicator of the sort of themes that needed to be addressed. Holmes (1995: 37) looks for developmental information:

> Despite the difficulties of categorisation, most psychoanalytic clinicians use some sort of developmental schema as a way of understanding patients diagnostically, indicating the severity of their problems and as a guide to treatment and prognosis. Despite differences in terminology and metapsychological assumptions there is much 'common ground' . . . depending on whether their problems are predominantly based on Ego, Object Relations, Self or Drive. I like to work from the surface depthwards and to be guided by the 'present transference' . . . rather than attempting complex reconstruction of the past.

Holmes' consideration of the ways in which attachment style affects the potential for satisfactory work between a clinician and a patient may be helpful, but most clinicians will have a scarcely articulated understanding of how each person will or will not be able to work. Usually the patient is very well aware of this and will not choose to continue to work with a clinician who is not a good match. Sadly, the patient is not infallible, and there are too many cases of therapy dragging on in an unproductive or even harmful relationship. Ultimately, the clinician is in a better position to make the judgement than the desperate and eager patient, and it is her responsibility to make it carefully.

How to make this judgement is therefore of the utmost importance. The traditional method is to make use of a trial interpretation. The clinician listens for an account of the present situation: what brought you here now? This is usually followed by an account of the history: what brought you to the state you are in today? Both of these areas will offer opportunities to make a synthesis, to draw out parallels between the past and the present, and above all to try to say something to the patient that he has not already thought of for himself. If the clinician manages to say something surprising, the patient will show how he reacts to being destabilised.

When the clinician has been with the patient for long enough – maybe one session, maybe several – she can begin to frame a hypothesis. This answers the question: what is the matter with this person?

For most analytic practitioners the hypothesis will relate to the way in which the patient deals with pain through some form of repression. This concept, bequeathed to us by Freud, has been fundamental to psychoanalytic therapies of all kinds. Desires conflict with each other and with all the apparatus of conscience. When they do so, the psyche has a mechanism to repress the awareness of the desires and of the pain caused by the conflict. The necessary corollary of this concept is that repression itself can become problematic. Defences are set up and symptoms appear. At the very least there is anxiety. In the *New Introductory Lectures* (1932), Freud distinguished between 'realistic anxiety' and 'neurotic anxiety' (p. 114). Realistic anxiety in the face of danger involves a state of preparedness and increased motor tension. The best outcome is that the tension can be resolved in action: fight or flight. In a first session there is some realistic anxiety in the sense that this is an unknown situation of vulnerability.

The clinician must find a way to distinguish this realistic anxiety from the neurotic anxiety which is left over from past trauma. She will have an impression of the way in which the patient deals with his anxiety, and Freud distinguished three manifestations. First is general apprehensiveness, which is a background emotional state waiting to attach itself to any new experience. Second, there is apprehensiveness which is already attached firmly to one source – in other words, a phobia. Third, there is the anxiety that accompanies the more severe neuroses, such as hysteria, in which there may be panic attacks and brief manifestations of anxiety as well as more enduring symptoms, such as paralysis.

The clinician is also subject to anxiety and will not be exempt, particularly in the first session, from the general background anxiety which is a signal of preparedness for the unknown. Each new patient is a source of anxiety and rightly so. Yet, the combined anxiety of patient and clinician creates a tension in which something *must* happen. In Jung's terms, the alchemical crucible in which two elements are melted down enables the formation of an entirely new combination. There is always the possibility that the alchemist may find gold, but even if she does not, something new and, we can hope, better will emerge.

4

CONTRACTING: HOW DO
WE MEAN TO GO ON?

A patient entering therapy offers himself to the unknown. The clinician does so too, but she should have a better idea of what is likely to happen than the patient because of her training and her own analytic therapy. In any case she is responsible for setting out the parameters along which and within which she will work. Whether any kind of agreement over how to proceed is possible is the subject of this chapter. There will be at least two and maybe more agreements that will change and be modified over time. The assessment session may be a one-off event and therefore it needs a contract of its own. The patient should be told how long the session can be, what it will cost, what the session could achieve, and how near he will be to a definite contract for ongoing therapy. This will model openness and honesty. It also raises the question: can the patient negotiate with another?

As attachment theory and the discoveries of the neuroscientists tell us that the early stages of development are formative for the ability to relate, we must assume that the early stages of the therapeutic relationship will be crucial in enabling a new pattern of relating to occur. The patient knows that the contract matters. Every patient who is beginning work with a psychoanalyst or psychotherapist is likely to want to know what is to come. Some clinicians try to make clear as best they can what is on offer and what is not. The problem for most analytic clinicians is that they genuinely do not know (and should not know) what the work will entail or how long it will take. Such questions are inherently answerable only through the process of the work itself. Yet, these are the questions that patients will ask.

The contract is of vital importance to therapy, not only because the patient is entitled to know at least the practical details of the treatment he is being offered, but also because the environment of therapy can affect its outcome. Alan Schore (2003: 45) quotes Rotenberg:

> The importance of the emotional relationships between psychotherapist and client can be explained by the restoration in the process of such relationships of . . . right hemispheric activity. In this way the emotional relationships in the process of psychotherapy are covering the deficiency caused by the lack of emotional relations in early childhood.

Setting out conditions and limits for the therapy ensures that the work of the clinician will have its best chance of being useful. It also allows the patient to show how he faces negotiation with another over his own desires and how he locates them in relation to hers.

Freud (1913) in his paper *On Beginning the Treatment* discusses the value of a trial period of two or three weeks in which to find out whether the case is a suitable one for psychoanalysis. He is clear that all that is needed at this stage is that the patient should be encouraged to talk, while the analyst says very little except what is necessary to encourage the continuation of the talking. A direction for the treatment will, in this way, be established by the patient. Freud also recognised the importance of the context or environment in which the patient will be able to talk, and he began with questions of time and money. In terms of time he recommends 'leasing a particular hour'. This is the basis for the analytic practice of requiring patients to pay for their hour whether they are actually present for it or not. Regularity is part of the reliability that we offer and Freud recommended that one should see all patients once a day, six days a week. He does allow for some flexibility. When a treatment is being wound up, three times a week may be sufficient. At the beginning, anything less than daily appointments will allow for a backlog of daily events if one is trying to keep pace with the patient's real life.

Freud had already thought of most of the arguments produced by new trainees who find these boundaries difficult to enforce. The patient will be prevented from attending through all sorts of ailments and accidents. Should he be made to pay for his session? Yes, he should is Freud's uncompromising answer. The analyst is making his living and cannot be at the mercy of whatever accidents may arise. There are also the problems that arise from the patient's resistance. A difficult session in which new material or a new transference situation is arising will tempt the patient to absent himself from the next session. Of course he may do so if he wishes, but Freud found that this happened much less frequently if the session had to be paid for in any case. He was not merciless, only practical:

> In cases of organic illness, which after all, cannot be excluded by the patient's having a psychical interest in attending, I break off the treatment, consider myself entitled to dispose elsewhere of the hour which becomes free, and take the patient back again as soon as he has recovered and I have another hour vacant.
>
> (1913: 127)

In answer to questions about how long an analysis will be likely to take, Freud quotes the philosopher who when asked how long a certain journey would take, replied only 'Walk!' He could not answer the question until he knew the length of the stride. Neurotics, as Freud says, are inclined to alter the length of their stride, sometimes moving fast, sometimes slowing down to what appears to be a standstill, giving rise to complaints from clinicians of being 'stuck' and to the jargon term 'stuckness' which, like the condition it purports to describe, is to be avoided *at all costs*. The conclusion that we reach is that *analysis takes however long it takes*. Freud said that it might take long periods of time, even as much as six months. He was a pioneer, convincing the middle classes of Vienna that money spent on analysis might be well spent.

Setting the fee will frame the treatment and determine the nature of the context in which the work is begun. Adam Smith (1776) analysed the part played by the division of labour in social and economic growth. Linked to the division and sharing of labour is the process of development of the symbolic value of money. In our earliest exchanges, the mother gives milk and love in exchange for peace of mind. If she does not feed her baby the crying will not stop. She may feel that her image of herself as a good mother is enhanced when she sees a contented baby. Later the baby will begin to play his own part in the exchange, offering smiles and love in return. Many clinicians have some problems with exchanging their services for money. What we do is not equivalent to the services of a plumber, although clearing out the blockages in the pipes may sometimes form a useful symbolic equation:

> Psychoanalysis is more than merely one of the myriad of
> goods and services which a metropolitan economy gener-
> ates for its citizens . . . Why is money here any more
> contentious than it is in the world of antique dealing . . .
> whose followers all recognise that their passion and its
> accoutrements have to be paid for in one way or another?
> (Rustin 2001: 174–5)

Psychoanalysis itself provides the critique of its own value. Each
patient works at acquiring the tools which will enable him to make
a better choice about whether or not to continue to spend money
on his therapy, especially the fees for missed sessions. At the same
time, via her fees the therapist will be able to demonstrate that she
is not ashamed of her own needs and that she can see the value of
what she is offering.

Decisions must be made about the amount of the fee and the
way in which payment will be made. Wisely, Freud begins with the
matter of discussion and negotiation of fees which most analysts
find difficult. The analyst will be 'frank and expensive', because she
has at her disposal methods of treatment which can be of use.
Analysts will, Freud thinks, have analysed their own anal repression and will then be able to speak freely. Do not worry about
charging a high fee; it will add to the respect for the treatment. In
any case, 'Nothing in life is so expensive as illness and foolishness'
(Freud 1913: 179).

Jane Haynes and Jan Wiener (1996: 15) do not think that the
analyst can usually be assumed to have sufficient control of her
own response to money. They ascribe this in part to the lack of
discussion about the use of money in most training courses:

> We discovered that neither of us are [sic] at ease with our
> own attitudes and behaviour in relation to money. Money
> itself is a technical means of exchange which allows certain
> connections and professional relationships to take place . . .
> the introduction of the national lottery has re-evoked the
> energy of a collective delusional fantasy of the crock of
> gold at the end of the rainbow . . . the crock of gold is
> often disappointing.

These authors recognise that analysts are likely to have problems
with charging enough but not too much. They point out that this
means dealing with one's own greed and shame because the most

dangerous situation is when the analyst is not aware of her own emotional connections. They conclude that she must charge enough to meet her own needs. The analyst who does not do so will begin to resent the patient and this will be disastrous for the outcome of the therapy. The owl and the pussycat made sure that they took enough money for the journey as well as the necessary honey (Haynes and Wiener 1996: 24).

Patients must therefore be told how much they are to pay and when they will be given a bill. If the bill is generally given in the last week of the month or in the first week of the following month, this should be made clear at the outset. Future difficulties can be avoided in some cases if patients are asked at the outset to bring their cheque in the following week. One of the reasons for saying this overtly is that any departure can then be seen as a communication about pathology and shows less interference from other people's analysts' practice, the media etc. Departures can also then be recognised by the patient *as* departures since a clear frame has been given. Complaints from patients indicate that it is also wise to say at this point that fees are reviewed annually and can be discussed at any time. Without this, some patients have taken the setting of the initial fee as a promise that it will remain the same for the duration of the therapy and have made a formal complaint at a future increase.

Analysts are aware that they are subject to the same unconscious processes in relation to money as their patients. They too will experience the effect of their oral and anal longings and satisfactions on their attitude to money. We all encounter in ourselves the same inconsistency, prudishness and hypocrisy. The analyst's task is to model a more frank and open way of talking about and negotiating money matters. Freud advocated a fee which would not be exorbitant but which would recognise the value of the work and the effort that must be put into it by the analyst. He deplores any attempt to play the role of the disinterested philanthropist. One of the dangers of doing so is that the analyst may be secretly aggrieved or may complain about the desire for exploitation or abuse in her patients.

Freud was opposed to offering free treatment under any circumstances. He acknowledged the tradition among physicians of offering free treatment to colleagues or their families, but said that not paying would actually damage the potential of the work. For a young woman it increases the dangers of transference; that is, she believes that the analyst is treating her free of charge because he loves her so much. The young man on the other hand, Freud thought, is likely to feel the obligation to be grateful which will remind him of any difficulties in his relationship with his father. Both of these elements could, of course, be analysed and Freud was the first to recognise the value of doing so. He also recognised that it is not the job of the analyst to produce additional transference issues through the reality of their behaviour.

The contracting process must address the length and intensity of therapy, at least to settle whether there is to be a time limit. Freud did not set any particular length of time for the treatment but did warn his prospective patients that if they broke off after only a short time, they would be likely to be left in an unsatisfactory state. Many analysts would also wish to embark on work with no end date. Time-limited work as it now exists was not envisaged by Freud but has become a highly respected and useful intervention as a treatment of choice for some problems (Mander 2000; Coren 2001). Freud's own exploration of the value of time limits is recorded in the case of the Ratman (1909). When the resistance seemed to have become immovable, Freud imposed an ending to take place within six months and was able to record an impressive unlocking of the process and significant improvement.

Many counsellors working in general practice for a physician are asked to limit their contracts to 6 sessions, but very often there is an option of continuing for 12 sessions or even longer. How does one decide, at the outset, whether or not a given person 'needs' more than the minimum number of sessions? In the climate of the early twenty-first century in the UK there is a painful debate to be held over how much should be spent on various forms of treatment. When people are denied Beta Interferon for multiple sclerosis because of the cost, how strongly can a counsellor argue for 12 sessions of her time when she cannot present any objective evidence to show that this will help more than 6 sessions in a particular case?

When writing about the formation of a contract for ongoing work, Jeremy Holmes (1995) bears in mind indications for time-limited psychodynamic therapy and puts forward the argument that all psychoanalytic therapy should be focused in the way that time-limited work can be, but that the focus should be continually changing. To offer longer-term or open-ended psychoanalytic psychotherapy, the analyst needs to be convinced that the patient has the motivation to continue and will not leave while the most painful emotions are just in the process of being revealed but before any kind of understanding has begun to make them bearable. That is why Holmes' criterion of motivation mentioned in Chapter 3 is particularly important. A history of beginning and dropping things before they are completed is always a cause for anxiety. On the other hand, when perseverance is raised in the assessment, there is an opportunity to discuss it with the patient who may well understand that this is one of the tasks for his therapy. The patient may then be able to work at his wish to end what will almost certainly be difficult for him. The clinician will understand that he has good reason for wanting to end his relationships or his courses of study and that therapy will provide even better reasons for wanting to end prematurely. What it must also provide is a still better reason for wanting to *stay* and get to the bottom of the impulse to quit.

Allowing more time may be helpful when the beginning involves a move from one attachment to another. If the patient has already met an assessing clinician, the continuing clinician takes on the role of a stranger who usurps the mother: something of the role of a foster mother or an adopting mother. She will have to allow time before she can be accepted.

A patient, Miss J., who had been with a previous analyst, came to see me. She had had a good experience, but the first analyst had been in training and when she finished, she left London. My patient was referred to me and came in a state of cold rage. I discovered in the first session that she had been brought up by a 'wonderful mother'. Mother and baby had been abandoned by a cold father who was remembered as returning in a martyred spirit to his original family after an adventure with a much younger woman. Because he had returned to interrupt the ideal mother–child duo, I saw myself at the time as representing the cold father who appeared in time to pay school fees and do his duty, but was not welcome or loved by mother or child.

Although my seeing myself as fulfilling the role of the father was in some ways useful, it took my eyes off the question of the maternal role, which meant that I missed some important maternal transference. This is always a vital area to address and will carry both positive and negative elements within it. My own internal contract with the patient was to work with the negative father transference. My supervisor at the time agreed and I deprived the patient for some time of the option of working with the positive aspects of her transference to me which related to the good enough mother, as well as the mother who demanded more from her than she felt able to give.

This case raises the important issue of the hidden contract between the patient and the clinician which is often formed during the first session. The hidden contract is the unspoken or even unconscious belief that each participant holds that there should be a particular direction and outcome for the treatment. On page 38 I mentioned the patient who had been told that he was borderline and would not make relationships. For the therapist, there must be a sense in which she does not accept this view although she may not say so at this stage. The patient will also have his own reservations, things he does not intend to say or emotions that he will not reveal.

The nature of the presenting problem must have some effect on the contract that is offered. Otto Kernberg (1985: 186) gives clear guidance on the treatment of the borderline patient in the initial stage of analysis. He is in favour of frequent sessions, two or three times a week at least, and thinks that this need not encourage a damaging regression if the analyst maintains a firm structure:

> I would consider a minimum of two hours a week as indispensable . . . What is potentially regressive in the psychoanalytic psychotherapy of borderline patients is the lack of sufficient structuring of the treatment situation and the related acting out of primitive pathological needs in the transference to such an extent that the transference neurosis (or transference psychosis) replaces ordinary life.

The kind of treatment that he has in mind involves consistent interpretation of the primitive defensive operations of these patients together with 'Control of acting out in the hours and firm adherence to a technically neutral position [which] protect the patient from excessive regression regardless of the frequency of the hours' (1985: 187). In order to achieve this technical neutrality in the early stages of treatment, the clinician needs to pay particular attention to firm management of the frame. Kernberg suggests that many patients are capable of participating in setting the limits to their behaviour so that the clinician is not left having to issue orders and prohibitions which will lead inevitably to a rocky path either through excessive idealisation or rebellion.

The case of the clinic patient is in some ways slightly different. Many clinics as well as some GP practices in the UK function through using some analysts who are still in training. If this is the case, the patient will be offered lower fees but the contract is likely to include a provision that the patient is expected to stay for 18 months to two years. As this is the length of time that most professionals would regard as the minimum for useful long-term work, the clinics can offer it with a clear conscience. In Chapter 9 I examine the effects of this sort of contract when the analyst needs to complete the two years because it is required by the training organisation.

Whether the clinician is a trainee under supervision or a qualified practitioner, both share equally the obligation to help the patient to vary the contract in whatever way is best for him, with only secondary consideration given to what is best for the practitioner.

Although there are some requirements and some prohibitions in beginning a therapeutic contract, there is still plenty of room for individual creativity and distinctness. Perhaps some training organisations have not left enough flexibility for their analysts. Charles Rycroft (1995) criticised the idea of inflexible correctness in beginning psychoanalytic treatment. The rules went too far in the direction of rigidity in that all power was to be given to the analyst. Rycroft described the old school of thought which decreed that a suitable patient must be diagnosed as suffering from a psychoneurosis rather than a character or personality disorder. If the assessing analyst declared that to be the case, then the patient could be sent to whomever was considered suitable or had a vacancy. The patient was to be seen as frequently as possible, preferably five times a week but four would be acceptable. The patient was to be told to use the couch and to follow the fundamental rule of free association. Fees were never to be modified and only the analyst's full fee would be acceptable. Any analyst, particularly a trainee, who deviated from this path would at least feel guilty and might well try to disguise the particular transgression from other analysts. Secrets in analytic relationships are all too easy to establish and keep, since, like some families they provide the ideal privacy and confidentiality for keeping bright lights away. Guilt may lead to avoidance of supervision and consultation which is a most worrying problem, particularly if the analyst is still a candidate in training.

All of these requirements and the possibility of varying them will be in the mind of the clinician. The patient will have his own power which may appear quite overtly, arguing about times, fees and the use of the couch or chair. For some people, the belief that they can resist the apparently great power of the analyst is an essential first step to allowing the analyst to have any effect at all.

> Mr N., a builder, comes to see a counsellor because he is having severe headaches. His GP has suggested that they may be connected with his relationship with his wife who is ten years younger than he is and about whom he suffers from feelings of jealousy. The counsellor offers him regular sessions at a particular time each week as is her custom. He agrees to the time but telephones the next day to say that a new job has come up and he will need to come in the evening after seven. The counsellor does not normally work after seven as she has young children. She is eager to see this patient and therefore agrees. He comes once more and then disappears, declining to answer her letters. She writes several times, realising that he has become quite a headache to her. With her supervisor, she begins to consider that he needed to test her firmness and to check whether she was going to be faithful to him. She was not able to fill both of these needs and would have found it difficult and inappropriate to interpret over the telephone. She did the best she could and he did not give her much opportunity to meet and work out what exactly was going on so that they could move forward.

A patient's acceptance of the therapeutic bargain may be provisional. He makes an agreement with himself to come only if and for as long as he finds it helpful. Even if he agrees to come for a while, his inner dialogue may contain something like: 'Well, I may need this now but I can give it up any time I want to.'

Patients have many ways of testing their own independence. One of the most familiar is the cancelled or changed session. This happens very often just before or just after the analyst takes a break but it can also happen in the early stages before the work settles. Some analysts will regard a request to change an already agreed time as likely to be reality based and will change a time if they can. Others will see a request for change as part of the ongoing work and will interpret it as an illustration of the patient's need to exercise some sort of power. Only after doing so might they accede to the change, if they ever do. Judgement is needed in this as in most of the decisions that we make. Can the patient present a convincing change of circumstance or is there reason to think he is demonstrating a desire for freedom of choice for himself? The power of the analyst seems great at the moment of agreeing to a contract to begin work and we should not be surprised if the patient immediately wishes to test the extent of his own influence over it.

The analyst is in reality in a position of some power at the outset. For the analytic clinician this is not necessarily a problem. It offers an opportunity to discover how the patient deals with the one he finds powerful. How does he resist or accept the authority of the other? Does he roll over with his legs in the air or does he begin a bitter struggle to subvert any form of authority that the analyst might acquire? The latter is destructive, as the former can be, but the latter leads to an inability to accept any help or any useful interpretation while the compliant response will lead to an over-eagerness to accept, but not assimilate, whatever the analyst says. Clearly both of these responses need to be recognised and interpreted as soon as possible because they will be toxic both in the therapy and in the life experience.

Some power-sharing possibilities remain but are a matter of debate within the analytic field. Legislation requires that the clinician reveal her record-keeping to the patient. If she keeps any kind of written records, whether hand-written or on a computer, she should make this known and either verbally or in a written statement make clear that she complies with legislation. In the UK this means the Data Protection Act and the Human Rights Act, both of 1998. The clinician must have a policy for allowing the patient access to any file that she holds about him during and after his therapy. She will have to allow him to see her records, if asked, and if the notes are organised in a form so that he can be recognised. Many therapists now keep very factual notes on file and are willing and able to show them to the patient at any time if asked. More personal notes of the sort that would be needed for supervision or consultation will most often be kept only until they have been used and will then be carefully shredded.

It is also good practice to say to the patient at the beginning something about the limits of confidentiality and something about complaints.

One of the main anxieties of a new patient in therapy is the question of the extent of confidentiality. He is about to speak to a stranger about some of the most difficult and vulnerable areas of his mind. He will probably have to speak about those close to him and perhaps those in authority over him at work. Occasionally information conveyed will have legal implications, such as for example the treatment of children or past or potential criminal actions. The possibility that the analyst can be trusted to hear and not to pass on such sensitive information may be something that will develop over time and cannot be forced. There is nevertheless a question about how much needs to be said in the initial session about the degree of confidentiality offered. In an agency, the statement may be something like this: 'Everything you say will be confidential to me and to [name of organisation]'. In private practice it is equally important to make clear the extent and limits of confidentiality. A statement should be made whether verbally or in writing that makes clear that there will be supervision or consultation – for example: 'Everything you say will be confidential, and you should know that I do have supervision/consultation'.

Some analysts would be reluctant to make this sort of statement. It may of course lead to questions about the nature of the supervision. Each clinician will have to work out exactly how much she would be willing to say about the name of the supervisor for example. Most patients are not concerned about the supervision except to be relieved that it takes place. Various aspects of the law could be brought to bear if a patient demanded to be told the name and qualifications of the supervisor. There is one important consideration, however: the supervisor has a right to privacy granted by the Human Rights Act in the UK and would have to agree to her name and any details about her being given to any third party.

New patients may bring new demands that have not been met before. The effect of a new patient on the clinician may be to provide an emotional shock. The acceptable course of action is to talk to a consultant or supervisor. Some clinicians use other methods of unburdening themselves: 'Why does an intelligent, capable and well trained analyst break the confidentiality that he/she has in good faith promised the analysand? Why do some analysts even though they don't mention names speak with indiscretion about their analysands in social contexts?' (Lander 2003: 891). Lander argues that the analyst listens to 'material as symptom' and is sometimes seduced into a symmetrical relationship in which she advises or explains. The analyst's role demands that she remain in an asymmetrical relationship in which she is listening and interpreting. If the analyst allows herself to be in symmetry she will be in identification with the patient and will not be able to forget the contents of the session until the next one. Clearly the analyst is obliged to develop her ability to be continent and hold onto her feelings until she is able to discuss the material with a designated colleague in proper conditions of safety.

There are other reasons for incontinence, particularly at the beginning, such as a sense of pride: 'Guess who comes to me for therapy'. This sort of pride takes many forms depending on the pathology of the analyst. Some may feel more pleased with more difficult patients and may wish their colleagues to know: 'I heard the most terrible situation today.' This sort of incontinence is rare but when it becomes a temptation, the analyst is obliged to analyse herself and her patient and above all, to stop it.

Because of the immense importance of confidentiality to the potential patient, the United Kingdom Council for Psychotherapy (UKCP) is, at the time of writing, producing a code of practice for practitioners, which includes a statement that it is good practice to make clear to the patient at the first session what degree of confidentiality can be expected. In private practice, for example, a statement should include whether or not the analyst has supervision or consultation. It should also include the circumstances in which a third party might be informed of the situation. Many analysts would wish to inform a physician (GP) if there were to be a serious risk of suicide and certainly should consult with a senior colleague or supervisor. The purpose of informing a GP would also need to be made clear.

Analyst: If I think there is a serious risk of harm to yourself or to someone else, I would inform your GP but I would let you know that I was doing so.

Patient: Why? What good would it do to tell my GP? What is she going to do?

The analyst in this situation is in an awkward position. What good *can* the GP do? My response would probably be that the GP may be able to prescribe or modify medication that could help if depression is severe. What I would think, but might not say, is that the GP can avoid prescribing unsafe quantities of drugs that would be likely to be damaging. What I would actually say is that sometimes a GP can be more helpful if informed about all the circumstances if a patient needs his or her help.

Patients may wish to avoid information going to their GP for various reasons. The first might well be the realistic one that medical records can be subpoenaed as can any kind of records that a judge might think useful in a court case. On the other hand, the judge can also subpoena psychological records from any clinician and the fact that a GP knows what is happening does not make it any more problematic. Doctors are bound by a strict code of ethics as are registered psychotherapists and counsellors. The General Medical Council (GMC) states that doctors must 'Seek patients' express consent to disclosure of information where identifiable data is needed for any purpose other than the provision of care' (GMC 2004: 3). Personal information should therefore be as safe with a doctor as it is with most of us. Frankly, the reason why clinicians generally wish to inform a GP is so that they no longer carry the responsibility on their own. Whatever the truth about the helpfulness or otherwise of GPs in situations where the anxiety of the analyst is high, the patient needs to know what might happen to the material that he will give to his analyst.

A second controversial area involves complaints and ethical codes in general. My own practice is to say to new patients that I am a registered psychotherapist, I belong to such and such professional body, I abide by its code of ethics and practice and I am subject to its complaints procedure. If the UK adopts statutory registration there will be no problem as everyone will be subject to the same national standards and disciplinary procedures. Until that time, the prospective patient needs to know what kind of clinician he is choosing. The practice of making a statement about complaints procedures meets with strong objections from many analysts and psychoanalytic practitioners and the reasons for this are various. The obvious one is that if you mention complaints in these litigious times, you might be seen to be virtually encouraging the patient to complain against you when times are difficult. This may be so in a small minority of cases although I cannot believe that there are many people who would not think of making a complaint if they felt that they had good reason. Good reasons are provided by bad clinicians and *bad* reasons arise from negative transference and can usually be worked through. If they cannot, the patient will make a complaint and the practitioner will have to trust that her professional body will be able to understand the motives and nature of the complaint.

One aspect of a clinician's behaviour, outside of gross misconduct, that is likely to lead to a complaint is lack of honesty or transparency. A patient may be driven to seek a complaint hearing in order to have a third party help him to say to the analyst: 'You are angry with me aren't you? It is not just my imagination that makes me feel that your apparent niceness hides a deep resentment.' The outdated concept of the schizophrenogenic mother may still have some relevance as much to clinicians as to the mothers of psychotics. At first, some clinicians might say in effect, 'I love you, come here and sit on my knee' while maintaining firmly that there must be no physical expression of emotion. Worse still, if you are of a school that encourages positive statements of regard or affirmation, you might say, 'You are a loveable person' and then refuse the patient's request for touching or holding, and perhaps even show disapproval of the request itself. The models that allow for ethical use of touch set their boundaries in a different place but nevertheless still impose limits. Whenever we touch we pull and push in two contradictory directions at once.

Some patients are extremely sensitive to the mood and thought of the analyst and can tell at once if they are being given something that is glib or textbook or just plain untrue. For the most part these are the patients who were at the mercy of a powerful parent and had to watch with care and anxiety every nuance of parental mood. They have developed antennae of great sensitivity and will prefer the most unpalatable truth over well-intentioned platitudes. Clinicians should not be indulging in platitudes generally but some forms of unconditional regard may be well intentioned but not true. No one should enjoy anger unless they have a strong and unanalysed masochistic streak. If clinicians try to pretend that they do not mind, they will cause more disturbance to their patients.

To return to the debate about describing complaints procedures, most patients in my experience appreciate the undefended analyst who is not afraid to say, in effect, 'I do not expect a problem to arise, but if it does, this is the organisation to which I am accountable.' Along with this statement can go something about how the therapy is likely to lead to feelings of distress and pain, but that what happens can all be expressed openly, in the knowledge that therapy is the appropriate situation in which this can happen. The patient is likely to feel much safer in the light of such openness.

A second reason for the objection of analysts and analytic practitioners to complaints procedures is that they will interfere with the development of transference. This will be discussed in detail in

Chapter 5. Paranoid patients raise particular difficulties in the area of complaints. Is it appropriate to say anything of this sort to a paranoid patient who can work what you say into something like: 'Why did she say that? Does she want me to complain about her?' Giving the name of your professional body to such a patient might open the floodgates. On the other hand, if a patient has so much need to punish you, he will find ways to do so whether or not you make such an initial statement. Probably the wisest course is to develop assessment skills so that the most paranoid patients are seen only in agencies where there is a sense of the presence of others and the patient does not feel totally at the mercy of one person. This kind of fear is the nursery and hotbed where the paranoid fantasies thrive.

Diagnosis can in itself encourage paranoid fantasies and is a dangerous tool whether it is expressed or kept in the analyst's own mind. Judgements in the form of labelling should not usually be offered to the patient, but will be made inevitably by the analyst. The contract that will be made overtly will usually relate to the presenting problem and the desire of the patient that has brought him to make the effort to come to a first consultation. Thus the agreement that is made will be to work, for example, on difficulties in relationships with a partner or at work, or perhaps on the feeling that life is not worth living. The analyst will usually have a genuine hope and expectation that this problem can be helped by psychoanalytic work but will also make a mental reservation. This reservation is to some extent an inherent part of the theory. If the analyst is to empty herself of her own desire and her own agenda in order to make room for the patient and if she is to avoid the trap of omnipotence, she must not be convinced that she knows everything that there is to know.

Two conflicting requirements face the assessing analyst: to be, on the one hand, the one who knows something about whether analytic work is appropriate and, on the other, the one who knows nothing but is willing to stay with the patient while he discovers his own path. Robert Hinshelwood (1997) emphasises that the patient who has a disturbance in his thinking is by definition not fit to solve his own problems or to know exactly what he needs. How therefore can he choose what sort of treatment will be best for him? He just wants to feel better and to take the quickest, easiest and cheapest path to that end. He may feel that he wants this or that clinician or that he does not want to be treated in this or that way, but society in general would ask for his reasons.

Presenting the patient with choices, in particular the choice about whether or not to engage in therapy on the terms offered is therefore necessary but it is also bound to be difficult for him. He does not know what analysis will mean for him and he cannot know unless he is willing to subject himself to whatever it might bring. All that the patient can know is how he feels with a particular clinician. He can form some sort of judgement of her statements, interventions and answers to questions if she has given any. All of this will add up to a general impression of something desirable, something that can be endured or something completely unacceptable.

Hinshelwood (1997: 34) points out that if we accept the concept of the divided mind which psychoanalysis teaches us is always to be taken into account, the patient may have a reasonable wish to have some sort of treatment or to work with a particular clinician but unconscious processes are always able to subvert his rational choice and lead him away from the person who is most likely to be able to help him change. The patient does not wish to change with his whole mind but with only the conscious part which may be relatively small and powerless. The unconscious is engaged with maintaining defences and particularly repression. The unconscious does not wish to know and will lead both patient and analyst a dance in order to avoid any risk that change can take place.

A respectful attitude on the part of the clinician leads to a wish to give choice to the patient. If there is a genuine choice to be made, perhaps we should do what the medical doctor would do: put the pros and cons of any possible courses of action to the patient and leave him to decide what to do. If we do that, we know that we are offering choice to a wounded or unhealthy mind, depending on the way in which we conceptualise the effect of mental suffering.

The end of the assessment process is implied by an agreement to continue with analytic work. That does not mean that there will be no further assessment. On the contrary, most analytic therapy is a continuing process of assessment in which the nature of the patient and his ill emerges gradually. The analyst must always be willing to change her assessment formulation and to be glad of the opportunity to learn more. The flexibility required of the analyst does not end there. As I pointed out in *How Much is Enough?* (Murdin 2000), on ending psychotherapeutic relationships, the most important criterion for a successful ending is that the analyst must be willing to allow herself to change in order to meet the needs of a given patient. The experience of the transference and countertransference will be an emotional one for both of the people involved and therefore there is inevitably a change process in which both must learn from experience and both must be willing to open themselves to something new.

Many clinicians give no instructions or help to their patients at all and wait to see what they will do with the session. I find that asking patients to say whatever comes into their mind as best they can is helpful because we can then deal with silence as resistance. Some patients are silent at the beginning after they have described their problem, simply because they think that the analyst is waiting for some particular kind of material. This sort of silence can usually be worked with constructively. Debates on recovered memories at the end of the twentieth century led to a preoccupation with the therapeutic value and use of memories. Some clinicians followed the precepts of Bass and Davis (1988) in *The Courage to Heal*. They advocated the recovery of memories of abuse as a way of curing all sorts of symptoms, such as sleeplessness for example. Analysts with reputable training and a responsible professional body are not likely to be seduced by such potentially abusive material. The effect on patients, however, is that they are often anticipating dramatic events which some might hope to experience because of the implication that recovering a memory of abuse will be all that is needed for the cure of all ills.

If a patient is unfamiliar with psychoanalytic theory he does not know that his benevolent analyst actually believes that he will have to suffer more in order to achieve improvement. A question for analysts to answer is therefore whether to tell potential patients that this is the case. One part of a responsible contract might include asking a patient about how he is when at his worst. This might involve checking out the degree and seriousness of suicidal feelings and impulses. It might also uncover potential violence. In this context, it is a question designed to give the analyst some insight into how depressed a patient is likely to become and how well he can tolerate the return of the repressed desires. This part of an assessment can give the opportunity for the analyst to say: 'If this therapy is to have an effect, it may involve some painful experiences and may mean revisiting some painful memories. I don't know yet what that will mean but you will have to be prepared to endure.' This is honest and truthful but clearly not very satisfactory because people are often looking for guarantees and promises. Those who are likely to benefit from the explorations of analytic work, however, are the most likely to be ready to acknowledge that such an imprecise warning is all that can be given and is the best that the analyst can do. The analyst's understanding of the suffering involved is in itself of some comfort and a denial or refusal to acknowledge the risks is likely to be far more frightening to the patient.

Nini Herman was able to trust her Kleinian analyst because he did not evade the degree of suffering that was inevitable:

> 'I shall give you an awful time . . . I fear'. I said the words dejectedly, on the sudden brink of tears thinking of poor RB again, how I had hurt him endlessly. 'That is all right' came the reply. He did not toss my words aside or seem to waver at their sound.
>
> (1988: 115)

Herman reflects that her analyst conveyed that he was available for whatever she needed from him. There is no brash enthusiasm for catharsis and no denial that what might be needed will be painful for both, but a calm acceptance that whatever it is, it can be endured.

Other models of therapy also show awareness of the need to give the patient some preparation for the task that lies ahead, even though it is not possible to say clearly what therapy will hold for any individual. Emmy Van Deurzen (2002: 34), writing about existential therapy, is clearly prescriptive:

> She [the analyst] may finally want to point out that her role does not designate her as a father, mother, brother, sister, friend, spouse or lover but as a companion and guide into the client's own way into the future . . . Thus from the outset the therapeutic relationship will be defined as a professional one where the analyst is the expert, consultant and employed by the client. The fee is paid in return for disciplined and methodical exploration of the client's way of life and living ability.

From such statements it is clear that patients deserve honesty from their analysts and that the best analysts will be soberly aware of the difficulty of the task but will be sufficiently willing to undertake it to enable their patients to begin.

There is other information that must be conveyed at the beginning of a therapeutic relationship. The UKCP wrote *Ethical*

Requirements for all its member organisations as one of its first tasks. It did so in the early days of its monumental effort to unite all the main models of psychotherapy being practised at the time in the UK. I was involved in writing these requirements and one of the most contentious issues was the question of what an analyst must say as part of the verbal contract and what might remain optional or be stated if the patient asks for it. The 2004 version of *Ethical Requirements* (UKCP 2004) states that details of training and experience will be given if requested. The other information that we have discussed about the analyst's accountability to a registering body and the complaints process to which they answer must also be given if requested.

Before an agreement to work is made, the practitioner must be sure that the existing relationship networks will not infringe reasonable boundaries of privacy and safety for the patient. Is it a purely professional relationship? This is particularly important in a small town or country area: 'Special difficulties arise when the analyst and his new patient or their families are on terms of friendship or have social ties with one another' (Freud 1913: 125). If an analyst undertakes to treat a member of a friend's family she must be prepared to sacrifice the friendship. We can all imagine the difficulties even if the friend is himself a clinician, when the treatment goes wrong or when the reports of what is happening are not satisfactory. Successful treatment on the other hand will lead to envy and all its unconscious networks of response. Boundaries are particularly difficult to hold if the relationship involves another patient or supervisor. The analyst must not reveal that this is the case doing so would break confidentiality, but must withdraw from the treatment on the grounds that there is a reason to do so.

Finally, contracting might allow for the ongoing evaluation of the therapist's practice, not only through her supervision but, at least in an agency, via a formal evaluation of service provision and outcome. Any forms to be filled in should be made known to the patient at the outset, as they affect confidentiality. The process of contracting is a time for the patient and clinician to assess the risks of intersubjectivity and to provide reasonable protection against a process which will affect the rest of both lives. The clinician is discovering what she can offer and is willing to offer to each new patient and has the responsibility of deciding what will be constructive and ethical as well as what she may be willing and able to achieve.

5

EXPECTATIONS: THE BIRTH
OF PATTERN RECOGNITION

The Jesuits are said to claim, 'Give me a child before the age of five and I will give you a Roman Catholic for life'. The expression applies equally to any form of organised belief. The early years of the toddler are formative times in which a belief system about what the world is like, what he can expect it to do to him, will gradually take shape. We have already begun to address the questions about the construction of the subject through the acquisition of language. Psychoanalysis rests also on the possibility of unearthing assumptions about the way the world is and the way the subject chooses to situate himself in it. Patterns of emotional response are built into the suffering of an individual in the present and the process of psychoanalytic therapy enables a repetition of the patterns to take place within the sessions and the context of the sessions.

In Chapter 1, I discussed the importance of neuroscientists' work on the establishment of pattern recognition in the infant. Attachment and recognition of significant others is a self-shaping process. Satisfying experiences lead to reinforcement of the behaviour that is satisfying. The process of analysis leads to attachment through good experiences which in turn build up the expectation of further good experiences. The experience of the baby soon adds detail to his initial ability to respond to the outline of the form of the human face. He learns to recognise the particular qualities of his mother's and father's faces that come to mean safety so that, at times, no others will do. Psychoanalysis enables the adult to question his assumptions about what is safe and what is harmful. The conscious and unconscious images of mother and father may have acquired content that is inhibiting the development of better relationships both with the actual parents and with others.

In their relational model of the mind, Safran and Muran (2000) have looked at some of the views of connection that have flourished and may have some bearing on the expectations that patient and analyst can have of each other. They begin with Sandor Ferenzci's (1933) ideas about unconscious communication which he referred to as 'dialogues of the unconscious'. He and Anna Freud carried out thought transference experiments with Freud in the hope that they could learn to use this technique to understand the patient better. For some clinicians this process has reached fruition through the theory of countertransference and, more precisely, *projective identification*. Melanie Klein described *projective identification* as the process by which a patient unconsciously rids himself of feelings that he would find unacceptable and instead is able to convey them to the clinician. This process has been seen as defensive, although Klein herself emphasised that it is also communication (e.g. Klein 1931). A clinician who believes that her emotional response to a patient in the first session is the result of projective identification must be very sure that she has examined her own part in her own feelings carefully.

Connections between clinician and patient may be less esoteric. Both patient and therapist have grown up in a particular culture, enshrining particular world views. The western Judaeo-Christian and Muslim viewpoints are the ones with which most intending patients will have had some contact. They will be the systems likely to inform expectations of physics, cosmology, morality and epistemology, although an increasing number come without any felt allegiance to any world view and perhaps discover that in fact they have come, as Jung suggested, to regain the religion of their childhood (Murdin 2000). The discovery that both patient and therapist are Jewish or Christian or gay might seem very important to the therapist but must be reserved unspoken. Assumptions arising from shared backgrounds can be as misleading as any others.

Lisa Appignanesi (2000: 119–20) writes in her novel *The Sanctuary* of the first arrival of a new patient:

> Through the window he could see the young woman emerging from the cab. He drew back quickly as she looked up at the house . . . He heard her running lightly up the carpeted staircase. Running up so as not to run away . . . She gave him a forthright stare of assessment then looked everywhere but at him as she took off her coat . . . The place had confused her. It conformed to none of her expectations. There was no receptionist, no waiting room, no double doors to allow for patient privacy. The carpet

on the stairs was threadbare . . . There was no arm chair placed in front of an authoritative desk . . . The room was simply an ordinary sitting room.

This patient was no ordinary first-timer in analysis. Nevertheless, the analyst behaves as many would. He simply asks her to tell him why she has come:

'Have you ever been in therapy before? . . . We may not suit each other. You can always shop around.'

'Shop! What would I be shopping for? Mangoes, apples, prickly pears? Is there a job description for the ideal analyst?'

Initially she has no intention of staying but she is convinced by his gentle willingness to let her be prickly and frightened so that when he offers to give her some other names she recognises what she is doing: '[her] voice was suddenly soft with loss. "I didn't mean any of that. I don't know what got into me . . . I'd like to stay and give it a try"' (p. 123).

Appignanesi illustrates very well how the patient brings some expectations but the interaction of the two people constantly modifies and changes those expectations. Expectations affect outcomes. The therapist at the outset must discover the patient's expectations of the therapy and must be prepared to recognise and analyse her own. In the UK the currently accepted cosmology that will be taught in schools and is prevalent in the various media will be the 'Big Bang' in which everything in the universe was created in one gigantic explosion. From nothing came all the elements of which the universe is constructed. Thinking of this explosion leads most people to a number of questions: how can something come from nothing? What, or preferably who, made it happen then? This second question leads back to the assumption that something was there before the Big Bang.

The human mind finds it very difficult to conceive of matter and energy appearing from its own absence. We are, of course, mentally structured by our view of our own experience. No one can know his or her own experience of being created but we all are sure that we know that babies are created by two parents. For many people, the known progenitor may be only one parent, but that is sufficient to be sure that there is always someone who went before.

As the child grows and his intellectual knowledge increases he comes more and more to understand the biological processes of sexuality and procreation and the expectation arises that he had a mother and a father and that every individual has a pair of progenitors.

Those who are affected by the cosmology of the Big Bang will on the other hand be prepared for something to come from nothing. They may have the advantage of hope that is less limited than that of others and may not hear the therapist say that there are limits to what she can do. One of the greatest difficulties of the initial phase of therapy is the gradual dissolution of the magical thinking that endues the therapist with the ability to make the world change for the better without the involvement of the patient. The hope that brings the patient to the therapist must be transformed into a faith that the effort required will be worthwhile.

Technology is increasingly a universal influence on the background of experience. Computer generations expect a response that is automatic and quick and attuned to one's needs. On the other hand, everyone who works with computers is aware of the rage that can be induced when the computer does not respond according to the human plan or does not respond at all. Both the therapist and the patient may fall into a set of experiences of frustration arising from an expectation of instant obedience and memories of the immense frustration caused by inexplicable failures of empathy.

The patient may demonstrate his expectations of relationships as he waits for a mechanical response:

Mr B., a young man of 27, was unhappy because in spite of success in his university career and having landed a good job in IT in the City he had no girlfriend and he felt that he was in every way unsatisfied. At the assessment session he was impatient with the careful summary made by his therapist who then asked whether he would like to consider if therapy with her might be helpful to him. 'No, no. I don't need to think. You were recommended to me and I just want to get on with it now. I know I need to do something. Time is slipping away.'

The therapy began and he turned up for the third session holding a book. 'This is recommended by a colleague who is seeing a shrink. Have you read it? I thought it might help if we could talk about it.' 'You're worried that we're not getting on fast enough otherwise?' asked the therapist. 'That's not it. I just want to have some sort of text so that I know where we're going. And maybe you're right as well. Maybe this isn't getting anywhere as fast as I had hoped.'

Mr B. is indicating several useful pieces of information here. On the one hand, he is much happier with a text than with a person. At least if they can both share the same text, there will be less discomfort than if they have to face each other with no intervening screen and no keyboard for him to use. The therapist did not make this interpretation at this point and in the fourth session Mr B. brought his portable computer. At the beginning of the session, he took it out, started it up and then looked up to say: 'I forget too much of what you say. I'd like to write it down.' Then as an afterthought: 'You don't mind do you?' The therapist was nonplussed.

She had been asked about taping sessions before but this was the first time that she had been asked about what she felt was a form of court recording. Her immediate response was to say, 'I think it's more important for us to think about why you can't remember what I say since you seem to have a very good memory for other things.' In this way she shelved the question and it was not brought back. What emerged immediately was that Mr B. had a belief that her words held a key which he always felt that he held in the sessions but lost as soon as he was on his own. Examining the sense in which this related to his past was very fruitful and led to his recollecting a whole set of experiences in which he felt that he had lost something precious before he could make use of it.

Alan Schore (2003: 30) emphasises the value of a cycle of stimulation and response for enabling a baby to develop affective structures. The therapist may echo the stimulation and play of the mother with an infant in her skilled listening and measured responses: 'The synchronising caregiver facilitates the infant's information processing by adjusting the mode, amount, variability and timing of the onset and offset of stimulation of the infant's actual integrative capacities'. Understanding this process would not be sufficient in itself to be useful but we also have the growing body of evidence that the brain at least is capable of continuing to change and develop throughout life. We might reasonably suppose that the mind uses the physical capacity of the brain: 'Scientists have been excited by recent findings on the degree to which neurons in many parts of the brain continue to undergo structural change not just through childhood and adolescence as was once believed but throughout life' (Green 2003: 7). Like mothers in the time of John Bowlby (1973), discovering their influence on and hence responsibility for the development of the baby, therapists are increasingly having to accept some responsibility for the development of the patient's mind.

The therapist may have residues from her own past which will affect the desire she has for her patient to achieve and her agenda for the patient to improve:

Mrs C. asked for therapy because she knew that her life was emotionally bleak. She had a good degree but was doing part-time teaching of English as a foreign language which did not fulfil her own expectations of herself. Towards the end of the first assessment session she said to the therapist (who was also a woman), 'I don't know what you think of me after hearing all that. I expect you've decided that I'm a bit pathetic. I've told you that I know I could do better. I just don't do anything about it to help myself. You probably can't help me if I don't help myself.' She had in fact described her family responsibilities which involved a husband who had experienced incapacity through rheumatoid arthritis. She also had three young children and parents who needed support as her father was in hospital. She had chosen the part-time work that she was doing in order to leave her available to her family. The therapist had in fact faced a similar situation when training in that she had two small children who she had left with a babysitter while attending her training seminars and seeing her patients. She had worried about her children but decided that she needed to train and that they would benefit in the long run.

As she listened to Mrs C. she found herself thinking that this woman did not have the spirit to take such risks and would need to work on her unnecessary anxieties about her family being able to manage without her. Mrs C., on the other hand, was confident that the therapist would be able to support her as

she supported her family. Her expectations were of the importance of support and her view of the world said that people
could not survive unless someone else took responsibility and
helped them along. She was gradually able to recognise this
expectation as it manifested itself both with her caring for
others who sometimes needed it but sometimes could do more
for themselves than she had allowed to be possible and also in
her relations with her therapist, who, she thought, must support
her or would be of no use at all.

For some people, beginnings need to include a religious perspective whether they have a religious faith or wish to have one.
Religious belief is not often mentioned in an initial session except
as a demand from the patient ('I want a Christian therapist') or
anxiety ('I'm afraid that you may question my faith'). If a religion
is known, it can create anxiety in the therapist because personal
faith is regarded in many cultures as not to be touched. How can a
therapist do her job if she feels that she may not enter certain areas
of the patient's mind? Like sex and death, the psychotherapist
treats religion as an area requiring great care and sensitivity but
not as forbidden territory. In fact, religion may encapsulate the
opposites of good and evil and have great value in enabling both
patient and psychotherapist to see the functioning of the superego
as well as the ego. For the patient with a religious belief system,
God is the template for the one who existed before anything else
and made everything happen. Such a belief encapsulates power –
the power of the creator and the wish of humanity to refer to a
more powerful and wiser parent than the ones we might have had
or the ones we could possibly have. The therapist is seized upon
as the representative of power, wisdom and benevolence and this
possibility also includes its opposite. The therapist might be the
tyrant who misuses and abuses power for her own ends. Finally,
she might be what is perhaps worst of all: weak, ineffectual and
unable to make anything happen. Particular circumstances of the
referral and the telephone contact may make one or other of these
conditions more likely than the others, but making one's way to a
consulting room prepared to pay for a first session implies an
expectation and a wish. The two may diverge but traces of both
can be uncovered.

The analytic clinician wishes as far as possible to conceal her
hand and wait to see what the patient's expectations may turn out

to be. She therefore makes some effort not to reveal too much of herself although the idea that one can be a blank screen has been discarded by most people as both impossible to achieve and as leading to an inhuman lack of response in the attempt. Charles Dickens' novel, *A Tale of Two Cities*, begins with his well known statement of ambivalence about the *ancien régime*: 'It was the best of times, it was the worst of times. It was the age of wisdom. It was the age of foolishness. It was the epoch of belief. It was the epoch of incredulity' (Dickens [1859] 1997: 13). He continues to employ statements of opposites for the whole paragraph. The therapist beginning psychoanalysis with a new patient must be prepared for opposites which may be present in a way that defies common sense. A neat formulation that implies knowledge of what is the matter and what the outcome may be is often impossible. The only valid expectation for the therapist is that the patient may always surprise.

Nevertheless, we do know some things about outcomes. Educational psychology has made use of a growing understanding of the power of teacher expectation in determining outcomes in the classroom. We need to examine the ways in which analyst expectations are formed by the referral and the initial session or sessions. In agencies where there are separate assessment processes, the notes on that session will inevitably affect the analyst's expectation of the patient. In one paper, Symington (1986) addresses the effect of analyst expectation but so far it has not been widely understood to be an important factor influencing outcome.

Teacher expectation affects the achievement of pupils. This is now a well accepted phenomenon in education. If a teacher accepts that a particular class is full of underachieving pupils who will gain few examination passes, the probability is that the pupils will fulfil this expectation and will not go much beyond what the teacher has expected of them. If the teacher has hope and expectation that improvement is possible, then improvement becomes more likely. The implications of this phenomenon could reasonably be applied to psychoanalytic therapies. When Symington (1986: 254) noted his own low expectation, reflected in continuing to charge a very low fee, and then allowed himself to think that his patient might have it in her to achieve more, he discovered that she could do so. He called the freedom of the analyst to change his expectations the 'X factor': 'the analyst's personal feelings have been shrouded by illusory feelings emanating from the patient's unconscious superego' (p. 262). In other words, the patient is deriving some benefit from keeping the analyst's expectations low. From the beginning, many patients will wish to present the most helpless aspect of themselves so that not too much will be demanded and the analyst will fulfil their desire for a nurturing, caring parent. Symington sees the act of understanding as located in the ego, but the false ideas are located in the superego. The analyst needs to beware of the extent to which the superego is activated by the assessment process when judgements are to be made. As psychotherapists we are obliged to be aware of forming expectations of each patient in order to be prepared to change them.

There would be small purpose in any kind of diagnosis if it were not allowed to affect the psychotherapist's thinking and behaviour. Once the decision has been made to begin analysis and the patient is attending the sessions, Wilfred Bion's ([1962] 1984) injunction to leave memory and desire behind on entering the consulting room for a new session becomes crucially important. Each patient must be greeted at the beginning of each session by a clinician with an open mind. However, openness does not affect the need for the clinician to prepare herself before each new session. Each therapist has a different personal ritual but most like to have a few minutes in which to sit quietly waiting for the next patient and reflecting on what he might need. This is important in allowing a sort of emptying of the residues of previous sessions and of the current contents of the psychotherapist's own life. These might be moments of anxiety in which the fear of what another person's psyche can do will have to be fully faced and allowed to come and go. In dealing with this, the clinician might think to herself: 'I am interested to find out what sort of person will enter the room today and I am waiting to discover how he will surprise me.'

The English word 'expect' is derived from the Latin *expecto* which means 'I wait'. The patient waits in the waiting room and the clinician waits in her consulting room and both are fermenting and hatching expectations of what will happen next. If the idea of waiting can be included along with the demand for the next session, there is a possibility of some space for the unconscious of the patient to appear.

Patients can certainly surprise analysts. As I noted in Chapter 3, diagnosis is not an exact science and many would have no wish to diagnose at all. The danger in a wrong diagnosis is obvious, but this chapter is concerned with the danger in an accurate diagnosis. The psychoanalyst who thinks that he is going to do only supportive counselling because the patient is too disturbed to take more probing work may well be offering the best form of treatment but must also beware of forming a judgement which will in itself limit what the patient may achieve. One of the most important effects of psychoanalytic therapy may be to enable the patient to learn how to analyse himself when he needs it. If this is accepted as an aim, it implies that the patient can arrive at being able to do what the analyst does. Patients with different sorts of pathology will approach this in different ways. Some clinicians will be delighted to see the patient grow and achieve the ability to analyse for himself. Others will fear their own redundancy which this growing ability to manage alone implies.

Patients will also have different attitudes to taking over the function of analysing. For many people, idealising the analyst is an important curative aspect of therapy. The neurotic patient feels impoverished and particularly poor in meanings. The analyst suggests possible meanings for him and to the extent that this is experienced as feeding in the mother–baby metaphor, the patient will resist weaning and being expected to feed himself. He will therefore use every means available to imply to himself and the analyst that he cannot do what the analyst does. He will fasten on any low expectations that operate in his analyst and will increase the tendency to be seen as low in resources and independence.

In addition to internal factors which emphasise low expectations, there are external factors that arise from the ethnic, social, cultural and family context of the patient. Ethnic factors in therapeutic partnerships have begun to attract attention. In the UK the situation has been similar to that in the other professions: white middle-class men and women are the psychoanalysts and psychotherapists and to a lesser degree the counsellors. Black and Asian people are still more often among the patients. Because this mirrors the power hierarchy in society as a whole it has not always seemed to be a cause for concern, although some training organisations have always included modules on 'difference' which include all forms of diversity, such as sexuality and physical ability. The UKCP has done valuable work on raising the profile of equal opportunities in the profession throughout the 1990s and up to the present day. The British Association for Counselling (BAC) did some work on the area for counselling. Farhad Dalal's book on racism (2002) makes a strong case for the need for psychotherapists to pay attention to the ethnic mix of the therapeutic relationship.

The recent history of racism and thinking about its effects should lead us to have some anxiety about how it manifests itself in the therapeutic relationship. Gill Tuckwell (2002) looked at the views of hierarchy in race that were prevalent in the nineteenth and twentieth centuries and points out that both religion and science were adduced to support ideas of hierarchy. She quotes Malik (1996):

> Scientific racism helped generate a hierarchy . . . that justified the superiority of the ruling class both at home and abroad. It proclaimed the fitness of the capitalist class to rule over the working class and of the white race to rule over the black. And it did so not in the name of divine will or aristocratic reaction but of science and rationalism.
>
> (Tuckwell 2002: 16)

Attempts were made in the nineteenth century, followed by the Nazis in the twentieth, to demonstrate racial differences based on biology through such characteristics as skin type or cranial formation. All such attempts ended in failure and few now would seek to promulgate such ideas. Nevertheless, the sociopolitical reverberations remain. When two people of different ethnic groups meet, the history of racism will be present even if the two people involved are consciously not willing to make negative judgements of each other.

Educationists have long been familiar with the white majority's need to locate problems within the black family or culture. A psychoanalyst can therefore wait and see what her patient will show of his response to the differences between them or she can address the issue early in the initial sessions. Tuckwell (2002) delineates particular kinds of transference that are likely to arise in the interethnic counselling situation and the general areas would apply also to the expectations existing at the beginning of a psychotherapy relationship where interpretations and development of each person's particular projections should soon supersede the general. She refers to compliance and over-friendliness, mistrust and hostility, ambivalence and denial of difference – specifically ethnic difference (2002: 67). These are all possible aspects of the countertransference of the psychotherapist. I shall discuss this further in Chapter 7. Countertransference may be a product of the psychotherapist's own experience and may owe nothing to the contributions of the patient, or it may be a genuine response to the patient's transference. In its strict sense, this is what countertransference should imply. Because race is such a powerful force in contemporary society, reactions and responses to it cannot be dismissed as wholly transferential, although the severity of a paranoid response may well arise from an individual's pathology and history.

Racism has many forms. The psychotherapist and the patient together might join in a collusive blaming of the environment. The patient is often eager to find something or someone to blame whether it is his poverty or his family or his education or some other aspect of his history. The therapist may agree that these factors are important but will not accept that the patient can abrogate his own responsibility. The patient's low expectations of the therapy may determine its effectiveness and could affect the outcome negatively. The first meeting will often be the time when the patient's own level of optimism will be apparent and will affect the psychotherapist with either some hope or a generally pessimistic view of what is possible. Clinicians whose attitudes are liberal in many ways may still need to interrogate their assumptions that problems lie within the patient's own history, environment or cultural context.

Children in schools have been shown to respond to the environment so that the difficulties they bring from home can be intensified within the school environment if it is not specifically designed to minimise them. In the same way, we would have to expect that the therapeutic environment can be either helpful or deleterious to the mixed race, mixed culture or mixed class therapeutic relationship. Such details as the opulence of the house or building in which the therapist works will made a difference to the power that the therapist is felt to hold. The furnishings of the room can have a similar effect. They can for example convey a middle-class attitude to art. Freud's consulting room showed his love of archaeology and of artefacts, particularly sculpture. Since Freud's patients were all rich enough to be able to pay him, he was not concerned about generating too much anxiety or envy. However, the therapist may or may not fear to induce envy of her own life but she might wish to recognise what she is doing and ensure that she addresses the effects in terms of reality as well as of possible transference.

Freud was happy to be seen as an educated man and was not particularly worried about the effect that this would have on his women patients who would have expected a professional man to be educated, especially a doctor. Patients in twenty-first century western countries are likely to expect a psychotherapist to be middle class and university educated. In fact, recent decisions by the UKCP have established that psychotherapy is a graduate profession and all psychotherapists will indeed therefore have a degree or equivalent as well as their professional qualification. This will show in all sorts of ways. There may for example be books in the room and the titles will demonstrate particular interests. My own room contains all my poetry books which are a reminder to me of my origins in teaching English literature and they provide me with moments between sessions when I might have time to read or reread something which has become particularly relevant. Sometimes I like to read a poem to fix my mind on something other than the previous session, although I am aware that my own unconscious will be guiding my choice and 'other than' is probably not 'other' at all, now I come to think about it. Yet, a poem can soothe and ease my mind, a feat which is often hard to achieve in the spare ten minutes between sessions.

I nevertheless have to recognise that my library will have an effect on my new patient who is looking for clues to orientate himself. He will try to interpret any details of my room as a way of sharpening his expectations of me. Perhaps he will see me as a romantic dreamer who is out of touch with reality. I may lose some potential patients because this judgement is made. On the other hand, more insidiously, I may find that some patients feel overawed or inferior because of my taste in literature. This effect may also appear when people keep professional texts in their consulting room. However, all patients wish to have a competent therapist and the fact that she reads the professional texts may be felt to be an advantage as often as a problem.

A patient came into the room and began by looking around at the books. I happened to have left a volume of the standard edition of Freud's works on one of the shelves. 'I see you like Freud,' the patient commented. This could have been ignored as a throwaway or social gambit which needed to be left so that the patient would understand that we were not there for social niceties. On the other hand, such a comment can be useful. Clearly 'Freud' will mean many very different things to each individual. He was the 'father of psychoanalysis' and might in many people's minds be seen as the missing father with whom the analyst communes in thought, particularly when the analyst is female. There is the implication that perhaps Freud needs to be in the room, otherwise the patient is in the unsafe position of being left alone with the mother, but no father. I could therefore say, 'You might be relieved to think that I have some support from a powerful thinker in doing this work.' Or I might say, 'Perhaps you are wondering how I might allow my thoughts to mingle with Freud's ideas.'

Comments of this sort made by patients may be very revealing and if we use them, can be valuable. What is difficult is that some of the responses will not lead to comments but will be stored away to result in further transference and will require uncovering work to be done in the future.

In addition to the silent effects of the patient's response to my room, I have to consider the shame that I might be imposing on the patient. Most adults have no qualms about admitting to their limitations in numeracy, easily saying things like 'I'm terrible with sums, pass me the calculator', but they would feel unbearably ashamed to admit to being unable to read and write. Why this difference in 'shame' between illiteracy and innumeracy? Will my obvious and perhaps flaunted literacy make it difficult for a patient to admit to his own failings and weaknesses? In our society, literacy is a valued and envied commodity – or perhaps I just see it as such because I have chosen a profession that above all depends on words. It is seen as a key to superior knowledge which implies power. In the therapeutic relationship the therapist has power of all sorts and one of the most cogent (though least recognised) is the power to speak. We must recognise that our very fluency and love of words may be difficult for some patients to accept even while they know that they need this in us. Fortunately in this profession, we are mostly aware that we are wounded healers and that the necessary skill with words must be balanced against deficits in our own self-esteem. Otherwise we will be unbearably smug and complacent.

Fortunately, fluency and articulacy are not the preserve of the middle class. Nevertheless, the desire and opportunity to train as a psychoanalytic psychotherapist might on the whole be limited to those with a level of affluence and education which is most often middle class. Training is a very expensive process and there is very little outside help available financially. Life experience is a pre-requisite, so most analytic candidates have a profession before they begin to be psychotherapists. They may need to work in the original profession while training and may find it difficult to decide exactly when they can let it go and become *a psychotherapist* rather than *a teacher* or *a doctor.* From the patient's point of view, it may be important that they are seeing someone who is wholly committed to the profession and the work they are doing. On the other hand, a psychotherapist is an unknown quantity to most of the general public who do not know how to place or relate to one and do not know just how enviable the social position might be. This is helpful in that it provides a relatively blank screen on which the patient projects his own images of the envied, hated or loved parent.

Awareness of the effects of her environment which may look comfortable and affluent or possibly poor and unable to provide adequate nurture is essential to the ethical and professional functioning of the psychotherapist. It is difficult to address, but perhaps still not the most difficult aspect of stereotyped expectations. The social and cultural reality of the racial dimension of the therapeutic relationship may often frighten the psychotherapist. Out of a fear of giving offence this reality may prevent her from addressing what is her business: the psychological effects. If she takes the trouble to assess her own feelings she may find a fear of giving offence since she speaks from the locus of power. *This does not excuse her from speaking.*

The major reputable training and registering bodies in the UK are obliged to abide by equal opportunities policies in addition to remaining within the law and they have made clear that there are penalties for failing to provide an open and unprejudiced service. Such injunctions may well be necessary but they will also inspire some defensive practice which may squeeze out spontaneity and creativity from the psychotherapist.

Most white psychotherapists need help from supervisors and consultants to deal with their own anxiety in working with diversity. Black practitioners have a difficult problem also in that the majority of their patients will be white. They will also have to deal with the surprise and perhaps dislike that they encounter: 'Oh, I was expecting a different psychotherapist.' At the beginning, the psychotherapist may be willing to address the issue of difference, but the patient may not.

A Ghanaian woman with a traditional head covering and long skirt comes to see a white psychotherapist. The white psychotherapist is not used to seeing African women, even in what is actually a modified version of her national dress, and is on edge and unsure of herself. She nevertheless does as she has been taught and raises the question: 'How do you feel as a black woman about seeing a white psychotherapist?' 'Oh that's fine, honey, I'm not bothered. I see white people all the time,' comes the reply. The white psychotherapist retreats and assumes that she can leave this issue alone now.

In a few weeks, the patient begins to speak of a woman at work who does not understand her and has made no effort to hear what she is saying about the way the job could be done better. The psychotherapist realises that she has not pursued the matter of difference to its root.

The root is: 'Can you understand me? How much do I have to explain to you?' The way forward is of course indicated by the patient: the job could be done better if only the psychotherapist is willing to listen to what is being said. This does not mean that the patient knows what is needed. The analytic therapist must assume that the patient attends in order to allow analysis of unconscious desires and therefore by definition cannot know what he desires. The only way to discover more is through the analyst's expertise with language and ability to hear what is only hinted, not fully spoken.

Questions will be raised by the patient, usually in disguised form, which the therapist must uncover. The psychotherapist mentioned above had to acknowledge a great deal of ignorance about the life in Ghana that was described and about which she knew very little. These facts were rarely the point and such ignorance was a useful way of redressing the power imbalance a little. She was able to say with complete honesty: 'There are things about your life in Ghana that I don't know about and you may need to tell me more if you think it is important for me to be able to visualise the places and the people. I may need to ask you more about what you say sometimes.' The patient was happy with this and in fact seemed to appreciate the psychotherapist's honesty and willingness to admit ignorance. However, patients are just as likely to resent the clinician's ignorance and the need to be told will have to be part of the negative transference from an ignorant and apparently useless parent.

Arguably, the first thing that we notice when a new person walks into the room is his or her gender. Not being certain of the gender of someone seen on a train or in a restaurant can cause unease even when there is no need for interaction. A psychotherapist meeting a patient for the first time will usually already know their name and therefore will usually know the sex of her patient, but she will not from that be able to construct the psychological gender. Only the patient can tell her that and it will take time. Increasingly the literature on sexuality lets us consider how complex is the construction of gender. Any individual has been imbued with the roles considered appropriate in current society for that sex. Some people of course have particular difficulties because they do not have a clear biological sex or they may have a degree of dysmorphia in which the individual feels that his or her body is not the right vehicle for what they feel to be their true gender. These people may need specialised help and will often have to be referred to a specialist centre such as the Portman Clinic in London. On the other hand, mild confusion or uncertainty about one's identity and consequent role is a common phenomenon in the population at large and is often part of what is brought for analysis.

Pressures to conform to gender expectations in education, training and employment can have consequences for both sexes. It can mean 'choosing' a career that does not reflect interest and ability, and for young women in particular this may mean fewer financial rewards. For both young men and young women, conforming to family and societal norms of masculinity and femininity may mean an avoidance of gender-contrary roles in the workplace. For some boys this involves the avoidance of caring, which not only has consequences for them (let alone for young women) in the field of employment, but also in the field of domestic responsibility.

Sex stereotyping is so obvious a factor that it needs little support, although there is no shortage of studies to indicate that it continues to exist. For example, both girls and boys make career choices based on stereotypes. So prevalent has this kind of thinking been that escaping from it is in itself a political act which may lead to over-reaction and to the therapist who does not wish to go along with it imposing an agenda on the patient. So for example a woman who comes to a psychotherapist wishing to leave her employment and find the courage to stay at home with her children might encounter a therapist who will mentally resolve to change this wish rather than wait and see how it evolves over time as a result of analysis.

The male patient has an equal but different problem in the limits imposed on his choices. Language is particularly harsh to boys and men who choose to act on their desire to be carers. Words and phrases used of boys who step outside gender roles include many forms of insult: 'queers', 'nancy boys', 'poofs'. The words have sexual connotations that imply failure to have sexual relations with a woman, emphasising that words are a punishment for betraying the masculine code of behaviour. The words themselves become an attempt to restore the power that the caring behaviour is felt to have threatened. Probably these words are used much more often by boys about boys than by girls of boys. Such symbols are used to legitimise rejection by the group which feels threatened by a boy's caring behaviour. Girls who wish to be engineers have in the past been mocked less systematically through not being taken seriously.

Men may encounter unconscious opposition in their psychotherapists if they wish to cross gender stereotypes, although many clinicians will have conscious attitudes which allow for wide variations in gender roles. What is not so easy for the therapist to notice is her own wish that the patient should achieve a gender role that is more congruent with her own view of what is appropriate to a man or a woman. As a supervisor I have encountered the need to help a psychotherapist to formulate a view of a gender question in which the solution is left open. As in all other areas of our practice a possible template may be set up through the work of the therapist but the detail of the content must always be filled in by the patient. This kind of restraint is difficult to achieve and requires constant work on the part of the clinician to recognise her own wishes.

Clinicians have other expectations. Since the therapist is the one who is supposed to know, the patient is constantly watching for signs that his therapist thinks that he has achieved a satisfactory life. Body details may be important in this judgement. For example, the therapist who looks tired or ill (or is in fact ill) will have to contend with the patient's anxiety and disappointment that nothing can prevent life events such as illness and bereavement. Few people would see a new patient while they were ill or an ongoing patient if they were seriously ill. On the other hand, some of us do work when tired and might be unaware of how old or ill we might look. A certain amount of white hair and wrinkles can convey an air of wisdom; on the other hand, a psychotherapist whose hands tremble with incipient Parkinson's disease or senility is not likely to convey enough hope to enable a patient to begin. Of course such a person may well be able to surprise the patient by her competence if an opportunity is given.

Age is an area of potential discrimination. Patients will have their own needs for a therapist who is perhaps not as old as a hated father or who is old enough to be wise and to take the necessary parental projections. The therapist can do nothing about her actual age but an interpretation about the need for someone of a different age may make it possible for her to be useful. On the other hand, the patient's age may have a great deal of significance for the therapist. A young patient may evoke unconscious images of the son or daughter who actually exists or who was desired. Clinicians too may form transferences to their patients that relate to parents and siblings. They should be able to catch and analyse these for themselves. Patients in the older age group suffer from the added difficulty that Freud thought that no one over the age of 40 could be analysed. Clinician expectations of this age group are likely to be low. Few would make a blanket judgement based entirely on age but there is little doubt that flexibility and the ability to make great changes will be limited in most people over 60 or 70. This does not mean that worthwhile work cannot be done with great rewards for both the therapist and the patient (King 1975; Segal 1982). Nevertheless, there is still something of an air of wonder which might have the slightly patronising air of 'Didn't she do well?' when an older patient has made good use of therapy.

Disability, like old age, is an area in which clinicians are likely to form low expectations of their patients. Those therapists who have taken the trouble to ensure that they welcome the physically disabled, even if disabled access is not always possible, are the ones who may have thought through their own attitudes to disability. The more extreme forms of limited mobility are likely to prevent people from seeking help except at specialist agencies. If a disabled or physically ill person manages to reach a psychotherapist, the temptation will be to ignore the disability or to overcompensate the need to treat the person 'normally'. This can lead to neglecting common courtesy and help when it is needed. Long-term disability and physical illness are difficult for therapists to address. Anxiety about an unfamiliar condition and its possible effects can be inhibiting. Secretly, therapists may expect gratitude for providing the kind of intimate care that is needed. The liberal therapist who tries to give all her patients her best attention may not wish to accept that there may be bitterness and even hatred of her normality. As with any form of difference or diversity in a new patient, the best opportunity is given to a patient if the therapist says: 'We need to recognise that you have X or Y condition and I do not know what effect this may have on our work, but I think it is very important that either of us can recognise any effect and acknowledge it.' Saying that will not necessarily make her task any easier in interpreting the mental correlative of the physical limitation. It will, however, help to establish the parameters that contain all thoughts, however unacceptable.

Since both parties are equally important in the formation of the therapeutic mix, the clinician's physical attributes and appearance need to be considered. What if the woman psychotherapist is beautiful in the conventional ways of the relevant culture with, for example, regular features and large eyes? Some male patients will find the fundamentals of body shape irresistibly attractive. Some women like to wear seductive clothes and short skirts. Is this acceptable or even wise in a therapist? On the other hand, what about the anti-establishment psychotherapist in long trailing skirts and scarves whose room smells of incense? Is that conveying too clear a picture of a political position?

Body image is a part of the psychotherapist's physical presence and may be as difficult for her as it is for the patient. The psychotherapist herself may be unhappy about her own body image in various ways. Like many of the rest of the population she may well be overweight. The patient who wishes to deal with his own relationship with food may find this difficult to accept. The actual body shape of the therapist will probably be less important than her ability to accept herself as being the way she is without denial and without illusion. Psychotherapy does not create the ideal and certainly will not help everyone to achieve any kind of an ideal, either in body or in mind. It may however help to achieve a greater degree of contentment which in turn may lead eventually to an individual being able to make changes.

Any personal physical characteristics that are noticeable will also need to be considered. I am aware of my very poor eyesight. I wear glasses but, when I am tired, my eyes do not focus well. I have to be prepared for patients who sit opposite me becoming aware of my poor sight. What will this mean to them? One person in particular was horrified by finding herself becoming attached to me. She became very anxious that she was with a psychotherapist who could not see. She accused me of being no good to her if I was 'as blind as a bat'. I was relieved at the image she chose. Some bats do not see well if at all, but they have excellent alternative sonar equipment with which they can fly without any difficulty and moreover, fly in the dark. They can catch their prey effectively too.

Nevertheless, I did consider that I needed to address her anxiety that she had acquired a psychotherapist who would not be able to see what she needed me to see and would not be clear or confident but rather blundering around incompetently.

So far I have addressed some of the factors which can determine the particular direction that the work of therapy might take when expectations are raised in opening sessions. Frequently therapists can find a way of attuning to the patient's experience, not necessarily by empathic words, but often by an unspoken ability to convey openness to new experience. Culture will affect some of the expectations that we have addressed and may also be relevant to some of the ways in which the therapeutic relationship can develop.

Women from the non-western world may be expected not to make eye contact with another, especially a man: 'In many Western therapeutic models, eye contact is considered essential to the relationship and avoidance of it is thought to be therapeutically significant. For some Asian patients direct eye contact is thought to be disrespectful, or in the case of women, immodest' (Cross and Popadopoulos 2001: 31). Freud himself wished to avoid eye contact and found it immensely exhausting to accept his patients' intense gaze for six or eight hours a day. This is one of the reasons why he required his patients to lie down. Many psychoanalytic psychotherapists would follow his lead in this, releasing both themselves and their patients from the whole question of whether or not eye contact is desirable. However, when the patient is on the couch other expectations will arise. The patient will hope for some sort of confirmation that the analyst is awake and listening which is more difficult to believe when she is not in visual range.

In this chapter I have raised questions about the ways in which the patient and the therapist will set off in one particular direction because of the expectations that they bring. This is not exactly the same as the matter of transference which I will examine in the next chapter, but if the therapist can make use of the patient's assumptions, she can attune her responses at all levels. She can develop the expectation that all behaviour whether verbal or not is a fit subject for an attempt at understanding and analysis. This expectation is the beginning of the process whereby the patient becomes ultimately his own analyst and is ready to leave.

6

TRANSFERENCE: THE BIRTH OF THE PROBLEM OF REALITY

Janus is the Roman god of the threshold. He is an ancient Italian god and there has been much debate over the origin of his name but one possibility is that it is partly derived from the root of the verb *dividere*, to divide. If so, this echoes the divided nature of the god who stands at the threshold. His image on coins shows two faces, one looking forward and one looking back. For this reason he is the appropriate god to preside over psychoanalysis. For most clinicians, the task is to improve the patient's use of his present in order to give his future a chance. In order to learn to look forward constructively, he must be able to look back. Janus was celebrated and worshipped because he might be able to make a mere beginning into a successful entrance. His symbols are keys and the rod or *virga* which the porters of Roman houses wielded in order to keep out undesirable entrants.

Janus was associated with the dawn and the beginning of the new day. He had connections also with returning, and prayers were offered to him for a safe return from a journey. He might be thought to preside over the rhythm of the analytic weeks in which the patient leaves and is already turning his face towards the next session and the time when he can return to his analytic work. The patient is likely to ascribe the *virga* to his clinician. She is to be the gatekeeper, the one who is supposed to know. Jacques Lacan (1973) said that transference is in operation as soon as there is someone who is 'supposed to know'. After the initial period when no one knows anything, the patient will begin to make his clinician into the cause of all the manifestations of his unconscious. The clinician will experience this and gradually demonstrate that the position is still vacant until the patient is able to install his own unconscious as the Other with whom he can have a dialogue. The clinician, nevertheless, has to take some of the qualities of Janus.

She must look back in order to find the threads that have led the patient to his present patterns and habits. At the same time she must look forward, remembering that the looking back is not an end in itself but is useful only in so far as it helps in understanding and improving the present. From the present springs the patient's future which is unknown and cannot be more than a guess for either of the parties to therapy, but must nevertheless be the whole justification for the probing and painful experience of at least some of the therapy.

When a patient manages to cross the threshold for his first session, he has already invested a great deal in his expectations of the clinician. He may have looked back at the recent past and found it unacceptable for one reason or another. He has looked forward enough to find some hope that the talking cure might achieve something for him. At the beginning of the twenty-first century, western culture as a whole is opposed to the idea of psychotherapy or analysis. This attitude may arise from fear of the unknown or from envy of those who have something which may be perceived as possibly very good, even if mysterious. Patients arrive with caution, suspicion or hostility. Some seek reassurance and some seek confirmation of their fears that the talking cure will not be any use to them. Each person will believe that he has a version of reality; either he knows that he sees it or he knows that he is out of touch with it, but in either case he is likely to believe that it is there.

Patients seek confirmation of their view of reality in different places. If questions of fact arise we can investigate the answer on the world wide web. The locus of knowledge is both elsewhere and all round each individual in the electronic ether. Ironically, the world we enter electronically is a virtual one in which questions of reality are shelved. Even entering the virtual world is problematic. We have become used to being able to summon power at the touch of a switch. If this does not work we are indignant at first and ultimately helpless in the face of complexity, which most of us do not understand in any depth. In addition the majority of the population is now computer literate and is growing accustomed to vast stores of knowledge being available over the internet. Increasingly, the accessibility of knowledge means that the professional has lost her mystique. We are all supposed to 'know'. I always look up any drug that is prescribed for me or someone I care about and would challenge a physician if I found worrying results. The psychoanalyst's art and science are also available for scrutiny although the public might have more difficulty in knowing exactly what to enter in a search engine in order to find out what their psychoanalyst is up to or should be up to.

One of the problems presented by the initial session or (equally often) by the initial telephone call, is that the prospective patient will ask, quite reasonably, 'What kind of psychotherapy do you practise and how does it work?' The analytic psychoanalyst might choose to interpret the anxiety behind this question and say something like, 'You are anxious about my ability to cope with what you need to bring.' There is an argument that the patient deserves a straight answer to this question, but how do we convey the theory and practice of transference-based analysis in a minute over the telephone? A brief response with the promise that the anxiety of the patient is reasonable and can be considered in the first session might be the most appropriate over the telephone. The patient may than take the opportunity to begin work on the past experiences that relate to this kind of anxiety. On the other hand, a response that is too rigorously analytic might reinforce previous humiliations and lead the patient to run away when a more considered response might have made it possible to stay and work.

The clinician will try to ensure that the patient will not simply withdraw in humiliation, which may happen if he recognises that the question is not welcome. If this is the patient's initial experience, the transference will begin to encompass the experience of having a withholding parent who could not cope and who defended him against demands that were too great by refusing to answer or discuss. In other words, the question will constellate the parent who says, 'Don't ask questions. It's this way because I say so.' Evoking this pattern can of course be useful as long as the clinician is genuinely not threatened by the question and is willing to look at the effect of her behaviour in an undefended way. Everything here depends on the patient having enough hope to stay a bit longer and see what the clinician will do to recover the situation.

The analytic clinician will have in her mind the concept of transference and will wish to use this from the first time she has contact with the patient. Taking the concept more broadly than Freud would have done, I would argue that it implies that all human beings, like other living organisms, learn to deal with expected repetitions of circumstances that they have already encountered. New situations are matched against existing templates and the organism seeks to respond with the minimum change to the templates. I put this another way in *How Much is Enough?* (Murdin

2000). Each new experience, particularly the experience of being with someone new, demands that the organism make a decision about whether there is possibly enough safety to stay and make a social or sexual encounter or whether there is a need for fight or flight. In childhood, each experience is full of potential pitfalls arising from inexperience. Only the gradual construction of a library of experiences – for example, that the woman who sometimes substitutes for mother, maybe a grandmother, is friendly and can be trusted not to do harm – will enable a child to make the necessary templates to trust the majority of people encountered.

A different situation arises when the child has to pick its way carefully round adults who are not safe to encounter. It must learn to find a way through a field that is filled with obstacles and dangerous holes in the ground. The next time it meets someone who is similar in some way it will pick its way round the same obstacles even though the new people will actually present different terrain to negotiate. The lumps and the holes will be in different places or will not exist at all, but the child will still be making the same circuitous or zig-zag path to avoid what it first learnt was there. Psychoanalysis gives an opportunity to understand that the obstacles being avoided by the neurotic defences are no longer there or are in different places. With eyes wide open the patient will be able to look at each new encounter and measure the way it can be taken.

In the early sessions of analysis, the patient will be demonstrating the paths that he has been accustomed to take. The clinician has the task of mapping the areas of danger that the patient is seeking to avoid. Interpretation will focus in the early sessions on finding out why the patient is alarmed or disturbed by a particular movement or form of words. Early interpretations will be likely to focus on anxiety, so that both patient and clinician can think about the source and measure the extent to which a particular behaviour is genuinely a useful response to a threat or is actually a response left over from the past which is no longer needed.

Mr P. had asked in the initial telephone conversation, 'What kind of therapy do you practise?' On being given the answer that it was psychoanalytic, he wanted to be given an explanation of what that meant. He would not easily accept that the matter would be given attention in the first meeting. He said, 'I know what you clinicians are like. You don't want to answer questions. You keep all the power to yourselves by not letting anyone else know what you're doing.' In his first session he did not refer to the telephone encounter but began to talk instead about his girlfriend and how unreasonable she was. Mr P. had been made redundant and had not yet found another job. His partner had a job as a teacher and was earning enough to pay their mortgage. 'I suppose I should be thankful,' he said. The clinician said that it sounded painful to feel that there was such an imbalance at the moment and that it is very hard to be thankful when a woman is in such a powerful position because it makes a man feel that he has no power at all. Mr P. agreed and went on to speak of his mother who was also a teacher and in his view much more intelligent than his father who had been very touchy and difficult to please.

In many ways and at many levels Mr P. was delineating the transference situation which will need to be worked out in all its forms during the analytic work. Few clinicians would miss such a clear message from the past, speaking of female power and male anxiety about whether the patient can ever satisfy his mother. Christiane Olivier (1989) has written of the small boy's anxiety caused by his love for his mother. He wants to be loved and admired by her but he is always afraid that his father is bigger and stronger and will be her choice as indeed he should be. The analytic task for those who accept this view of transference will be to track down the situation that did genuinely exist in the past but is no longer valid. Mr P. is no longer the small boy who was bound to be defeated by his father. Early interpretations will focus on making this distinction clear and will probably follow the lines proposed by James Strachey (1934).

Strachey set out his groundbreaking attempt to understand why and how interpretation of the unconscious meaning of the patient's statements and behaviour can be therapeutic. He based his view on the child's primitive superego which is cruel and demanding and makes the patient afraid of every internal command or prohibition. Such an approach puts emphasis on the transference as the projection of the patient's harsh superego onto the clinician. She becomes the embodiment of disapproval and rejection. Her job is to feed back slowly and gradually the difference between what she is actually saying and what the patient thinks he has heard. She may sometimes disapprove of him but the reality is unlikely to be as severe as he thinks. The focus is on showing how the present differs from the past when the child might have imagined or experienced the parents giving him orders and harsh judgements, like the primitive superego. More importantly it is a matter of demonstrating that the present reality is different from the patient's internal images of reality.

The difficulty of this view of interpretation is that it takes as a premise that the clinician has a more accurate or true picture of reality than the patient. While we would hope that this is so, since the patient is paying the clinician to have a clearer view of reality than he has, nevertheless we have to accept that she is not always reliable and that her own analysis is not always thorough. Even Lacan accepted that the analyst knows *something*, but he defines the knowledge as the analyst's desire that the analytic dialogue should continue: 'He must know. To him must be transmitted, through actual experience, what it is all about . . . it is what I designate under the term *the desire of the psycho-analyst*' (1954: 230).

The role of the analyst is different from that of the patient at the beginning although they may converge as time goes on. Although Jung's view was that 'the analyst should hold himself back in order to give his analysand the chance to play his hand to the full' (Asper-Brugisser 1983: 2), yet he points out that it is rare to find a patient who is easily able to make himself an object of observation. That takes time.

At the beginning the patient seeks to be able to convince the clinician that his own view of reality sometimes has some merit and in fact may be a useful defence for him. Mr P. might find that his partner does think that he is pathetic for not having a job and his clinician might not despise him for being unable to take control of his life. The clinician must learn the transference situation and must not be dogmatic about the extent to which the primitive images are or are not relevant. She must be willing to discover that she is wrong and willing to change her mind. If she can do this, she will be creating a new situation which she can then invite the patient to contemplate. In this way, she will do what Strachey recommends in that the primitive image will be questioned and not taken to be the whole truth.

In this situation the analytic clinician is working against time. Suman and Brignone (2001) discuss the development of the much accelerated pace at which we expect all aspects of life to be conducted. Babies still take nine months to reach the moment of birth and love still grows slowly over the years, but many people are unwilling to wait for the latter even though they have no choice over the former (yet). Other forms of change are expected to work quickly. Most visits to the GP result in a prescription for a drug from which the patient expects to see results in a matter of days, if not hours. Once an improvement is experienced, many people see no need to finish the course.

We cannot be surprised if therapeutic relationships often follow the tendency that we can observe outside psychoanalysis. If one of the participants thinks that therapy is no longer obviously useful to him, he may well decide to bring the whole enterprise to a swift and unilateral conclusion. When the patient begins to feel a bit better, the clinician may be thrown out. Many people are shocked to find that long-term psychotherapy or psychoanalysis is not available in any easy to acquire form and has to be paid for, often at considerable sacrifice. The resentment that this brings about may hinder the development of a working relationship. If there is too much envy of the clinician for receiving the fee, the patient is unlikely to be able to make use of what the clinician offers.

Each patient will of course bring a different version of what Suman and Brignone (2001: 467) call the *pre-formed transference*, but there may be some aspects which most people share. For example, the tendency to social comparisons will inevitably enter into the ability to form a unique transference. In other words, there may be a social norm which says that therapy is useful but, in the style of Woody Allen, journalists and film-makers mock clinicians as the prop of the inept or gullible. The kind of transference that develops in this case may be more infected with shame than any other emotion. On the other hand, the patient who has come because a friend or partner has recommended therapy may develop a transference which has strong elements of compliance in it because of the need to achieve at least as rewarding an experience as the friend or partner. Although Suman and Brignone (2001) call this a *pseudo transference*, it is no more pseudo than any other because it will in fact rest on the basis of other experiences and will repay attention for its present manifestation. It may well also allow for exploration in terms of past experiences.

Suman and Brignone designate as a *pre-formed transference* the cultural transference to psychoanalysis. Like most transference this has a positive and a negative pole. In some areas, particularly the

101

study of literature and history, the study of psychoanalysis has become a matter of course. The ideas of psychoanalysis are singled out for rubbishing by the press. On the other hand, this sort of attack shows (if nothing else) that psychoanalysis is considered dangerous and powerful. Its ideas are not always understood by such populist writers but they are clearly seen as a major cultural influence.

The changes that are taking place in our cultural context, such as powerful relationships with computers and information technology in general, are bound to have effects on the way in which the human mind works and perhaps on the way in which it is structured. Pre-formed transference is not only in the conscious attitudes of the media but also the general values of the dominant culture which are at present individualistic and self-centred. The shadow side of the father who is more available to his family, especially his children, seems to be expressed in a much greater fear of sexual abuse than in the past. This in turn will reveal itself as a fear of the 'father' clinician who can abuse the power that the patient is about to give to him (or her).

'At the end of the first encounter a patient tells a dream he had the previous night: a burglar was coming from the terrace of his home and the patient wondered how he could prevent him from getting in' (Suman and Brignone 2001: 466). The writers are making the point here that the obvious transference interpretation may arise from a culturally derived anxiety about psychoanalysis as well as from an individual anxiety about intrusion. In this case, there has not been much time for a unique transference to the clinician to develop.

From a Jungian perspective, the initial phase of analysis has an archetypal quality. In his paper on the importance of the initial dream in indicating the direction of the treatment, Maduro (1987: 199) emphasises the repetition of patterns: 'Analysis is a cyclical process with the beginning of one's life often returning to repeat itself as the central clinical issue'. In attempting to focus on criteria for analysability Maduro returns to Jung's use of the dream that the patient brings to the assessment or first session. He quotes Jung: 'There are times when a dream in the beginning of analysis contains the whole analytical procedure' (1987: 199).

The criteria for analysability relate to the symbolic value of the dream and the patient's behaviour in relation to that dream. Both of these factors may be taken in many different lights depending on the theoretical base of the clinician. Sometimes the dream may indicate a transference situation in which the clinician must beware of dangers to the patient and herself. Sometimes the dream may hint at the possibility of resolution:

> Mrs M. came to see a psychoanalyst because of depression and low self-esteem. She recounted a dream in the first session after the assessment. She was sitting on a man's knee and felt very safe and comfortable. Then suddenly as she was looking at him he changed into a skeleton. She leapt up and jumped out of the window and found herself falling with the skeleton in her arms. In the therapy that followed the picture of sudden change from trust to terror occurred with the clinician but more often expressed itself as over-strong attachment while a very positive, rather clinging relationship developed. The clinician was then able to say that she understood the anxiety that the therapist should not turn into the skeleton which would be a reminder of death.

To take the step of approaching someone for treatment will require a considerable act of courage or desperation and will involve the creation of an image, often idealised, of the clinician and her wisdom and ability to help. This leads to an initial period in which the patient in most cases is prone to idealise the clinician because he needs to do so in order to preserve hope.

Jungian emphasis on the collective unconscious leads to a consideration of the usefulness of fairy tales in understanding the formation of a particular type of transference. For example, Asper-Brugisser (1983: 8) describes a woman who came to treatment as a Cinderella whose mother had just died. She revealed that she was looking for a mother and feared a wicked stepmother. From the 'cinders' she will need to progress to the ball and find out whether the shoe of adulthood will fit her.

The recent *rapprochement* between psychoanalysis and neuro-science, a development which might have greatly pleased Freud, enables us to see just how complex the process of transference is. The ethnologist Nikolaas Tinbergen has become well known to psychoanalytic theory because his studies of imprinting in birds showed the way to further, more recent work on the development of the processes of thinking (Tinbergen 1951). Imprinting takes place in a complex manner in human beings and leads to attachment which is sometimes difficult to understand because it may focus on what is negative or destructive.

Frank Tallis (2002) set out to reinstate Pierre Janet, the French philosopher who began pioneering work on the power of the unconscious to transfer images from the past into the present. Tallis points out that Janet's work was generally ignored and overshadowed by Breuer and Freud (1895) and their *Studies on Hysteria*. In 1893 Janet published his 'On the psychical mechanisms of hysterical phenomena: preliminary observations'. He showed that he had treated hysterical illness and blindness by the same means as Breuer and Freud. Also seeking to understand the persistence of patterning, Jean Knox (2003) examined the implications of neuroscience for Jung's concept of the archetype and she arrives at the conclusion that archetypes represent image schemas. They are not genetic and are different from drives, but are the product of the infant's learning about the relationships of objects to each other in space. This is not instinctual but is sufficiently reliable across race, culture and individual difference to be regarded as universally human. These schemas are elaborated by the process of symbolism.

The human infant relates to its early objects with love and hate. These objects become the central points of schemas in which love and hate are the emotional poles. As other experiences accrete, each set of experiences grows and attracts to itself new experiences. An analytic clinician is happy to be drawn into a set of experiences because from this vantage point she can understand something of the reasons why the patient is suffering. This attitude is possible only thanks to Freud's discovery of the concept of transference and is still the main tool for the analytic schools of therapy.

Freud discovered the power of infantile love and hate through the difficult experience of his colleague, Joseph Breuer, whose hysterical patient, Anna O (Bertha Pappenheim) fell in love with him and produced a phantom pregnancy (Breuer 1895). Freud (1915) then became interested in transference as the displacement of affect and was relieved to be able to write his paper *Observations on Transference Love* in which he was able to say that the woman who falls in love with her clinician does so only because she is repeating an unremembered experience of the past. From its earliest beginnings as the identification and understanding of a problem, transference has mutated into one of the most powerful therapeutic tools of the analytic therapies. It is more convincing as a pragmatically useful technique than for the explanatory power that Freud hoped that it would have. Critiques such as that of David Livingston Smith (1991) have shown some of the difficulties with the concept, but it remains of great practical value. As I suggested in Chapter 3, indications of the kind of transference that is developing may well be used as an important aspect of diagnosis. A delusional transference which the clinician will find hard to endure may be a good reason to pass the patient on to another clinician or to suggest that analytic therapy is not appropriate in a particular case.

Examples of delusional transference are not difficult to find. Experience teaches that a patient who arrives for an assessment interview with a strongly negative parental image in front of him, may not be able to see that the clinician might be helpful given time. He is not likely to benefit from analytic therapy because of the need to work in and through the existing relationship. This kind of difficulty can be seen in George:

George came to his first consultation saying that his problem was that he could no longer find any enjoyment in his work as a salesman of IT systems. He was 43 and until six months ago had been a very good salesman, one of his company's best. His figures were now slipping and he actively disliked both his colleagues at work and his customers. Clearly, he could not continue as he was but he could not imagine finding any other work at his age. He said 'I'm finished, aren't I?', for a moment revealing his despair. The psychoanalyst was able to feel a connection with him and to feel some empathy with his sense of hopelessness. This did not last long because he looked at her and said, 'I don't know why I'm telling you this. I can see that you think I'm all washed up. You have a triumphant look that I recognise. I know that look. My mother looked just like that when I failed an exam. It makes you feel good doesn't it? You need patients who are in a bad state, worse off than you because that lets you feel better. I know what you're up to and I can't stop you enjoying my problems. Maybe I even want you to.'

The clinician feels trapped. Clearly the patient has decided that he wants therapy with her but if she takes him on it will be to struggle with a destructive structure in the patient which will bring out any tendency to sadism in herself.

Such a perverse structure involves a disavowal. For George, the disavowal of the possibility of castration is clear. He recognised that the woman had phallic power in that she was able to triumph over him. He then managed to ignore his own fear of losing his phallus by acquiescing to the woman's power which in itself was an illusion. Sharing with her in an illusion sets up a potential collusion which the clinician is constantly required to join. George kept himself from recognising the loss either of his own power or the woman losing hers. If she can lose hers, this leads the man back to the possibility of losing his own.

Although such a transference state would place great demands on the clinician's ability to retain her own view and understanding of what is happening, it might still be possible to work with it in terms of unbinding the patient from repeating his pain. Freud understood that transference arises from the need to repeat. The principle that he stated is that the patient does not remember; the patient repeats. He implied of course that remembering would be better than repeating. The energy bound up in the unconscious need to repeat the painful scenario becomes available to the ego if the painful experience can be remembered and thus be available for expression in words. Since in this model, repetition holds the patient in the structure of the pleasure principle, pending movement to the reality principle, Freud was in the business of arguing that painful repetition is actually pleasurable. Ellie Ragland (1995: 88) emphasises that Lacan recognised this impasse and found a way beyond it:

> We are not driven towards death as entropy. Rather we are driven by 'death' in the form of excesses in *jouissance*. That is, we cling to fetish objects (object *a*) which we identify as our Good. Humans remain locked in double binds for no apparent reason, unhappy as if on purpose. The reason is not mysterious in Lacan's teaching. We are controlled by traumatic events that have already constituted the real as an order of meaning that remain nonetheless in thought, memory or the body as blockages. Traumatic material is unsymbolized knowledge which is present as knots or suspended impasses in language (thought).

Ragland's observations have implications for the path that can be taken, for the direction of the treatment. If we seek to repeat what is painful, that is not because we seek death or dissolution as such but because we seek the pleasure of pain itself and the constancy of that familiarity. The patient arriving for therapy is therefore *bound* to repeat, not just to show the nature of the symptom but also to give himself the satisfaction of being bound to his own *jouissance*. At first reading this can sound very similar to Freud's theory of the death instinct seeking to return all flesh to the stasis and inanimate state from which it originally came. In fact, Lacan was saying that the purpose of seeking repetition and *jouissance* was to protect the individual from knowledge, and the knowledge that we most dread is hinted in the gaps where the unconscious makes its presence felt. If these holes or gaps are recognised by the clinician, the patient cannot indefinitely protect himself from knowledge of loss.

The patient on the doorstep has brought not only his need for competence and goodwill in the clinician, but also his mindset and the object of desire to which he is bound. Knowledge may be acquired intellectually and may sometimes help, but for the patient who comes to us such methods have not been enough or have not worked well enough.

Matte Blanco (1988), a Chilean psychoanalyst, examined the nature of the Freudian unconscious in mathematical and logical terms. He discussed the problems of thinking about what is essentially unknowable and suggested that we can deal with this difficulty in one of the ways that we deal with mathematical problems – in terms of sets:

> We may therefore legitimately conclude that the present mathematical concept of the infinite is only a substructure of the logic of the unconscious, seen as a set of bi-logical structures; and also is a substructure of any symmetrised set formed of whatever number of whatever objects.
>
> (1988: 69)

Blanco claims that the qualities of the unconscious do allow for conceptualisation through set theory and that conceptualised sets may contain whole or part objects. What is particularly interesting from the point of view of understanding transference is that:

> In mathematical reasoning about the infinite, equinumerosity is the only property in which the proper part and the whole are treated as identical. In fact a simple reasoning

which I shall not present here, shows that if we accept equinumerosity, this leads to the identity of all the properties.

(1988: 69)

In other words, if you match two mathematical sets – for example, the set of all numbers with the set of all even numbers, you find that there is a one-to-one correspondence and, since one is infinite, they are both infinite:

1 2 3 4 etc.
2 4 6 8 etc.

In the same way, if you map the properties of two sets in the unconscious, you find that they can be matched infinitely. In the unconscious one can equal two and three can equal four: 'The infinite is the schizophrenic and the unconscious of mathematics, but also its poetry' (Blanco 1988: 68).

Blanco's concept of the essential antimony of human nature is also relevant to an understanding of the transferential process. *Antimony* describes the incompatibility between two assertions, both of which can claim to be true. In the unconscious, two sets can be equated and both 1 and 2 can be true at the same time. This is the basic process that happens when an alien from another planet stands on my doorstep and something about the set of its eyes is like that of a teacher who had terrified me. I cannot understand what the alien's attempts at communication mean and I am certainly not consciously thinking of the teacher, but I know that this is an alien and therefore a completely new and unpredictable experience and I also know that he is going to harm me as my teacher did. Two sets of experience are conflated in the unconscious and I arrive at some conscious behaviour which is based on totally unconscious identifications. My response may be based on my internal reality but may equally be an example of what Lacan (1949) would call *méconnaissance* (misperception of the ego).

As soon as the patient crosses the threshold, he will be looking to the clinician for a statement which will transform his state of ignorance into knowledge by enabling him to share in the knowledge that the clinician has. Strachey (1934) argues that the clinician must begin a process of building up the evidence to make a mutative transference interpretation. Such an interpretation involves seeing the gap between the patient's perception and the clinician's perception of reality. The clinician must know better than the patient how she 'really' is and what she is 'really' like. Unfortunately, if we accept any of Lacan's teaching about the tendency of the ego to misconstrue reality in its favour, we must also have some hesitation in accepting that the clinician can be relied upon to understand and reveal exactly where the cut falls between the world as it is and the view from the locus of the transference.

For example, a patient in the first session tells of his wife who is very loving and considerate. He thinks she is wonderful, but he cannot have an erection. She is perhaps too good, he suggests. He prefers looking at images on the internet. He does not specify what kind of images, but the psychoanalyst assumes that they are pornographic ones. She listens to his tentative pleas that she will be able to help him and moves straight into a transference interpretation that he might be worried that if she is a good clinician he will feel small and impotent. In analytic terms this might be considered a correct interpretation, and might be useful as a diagnosis of how he can respond to interpretation, which is worth investigating at the beginning of the work.

Lacan would, however, object to the assumption that the clinician has made the definitive statement about what is going on here. He points out that the transference interpretation will be heard to be coming from the person who is projected onto the clinician at the time. In other words, if the patient is beginning to project his wife onto the clinician and she makes a wise statement which shows perception, she will be heard as already too wise and knowledgeable and the only possible response will be to demonstrate his usual reaction to his wife.

The first session is an opportunity to begin to map the patient's sets of experience. An entire set is immensely powerful in determining what my response will be when I meet the alien from another planet on my doorstep, and equally when I open the front door to encounter a new neighbour. I may anticipate something good and positive as the most likely outcome of the encounter. I may be eager to find out what this alien has to tell me and I may interpret the way it waves its tentacles at me as a conciliatory gesture implying a wish for friendship: a sort of handshake impulse. Alternatively, if my set of experiences has been predominantly negative, if I have often been hurt and my trust has been betrayed, I am of course likely to respond to the alien with suspicion. I will not interpret tentacle-waving in a favourable way but will anticipate that the creature is trying to grab me for some evil purpose.

Each of us has a set of experiences that might consist of infantile or two-person relationships. This set will include the dyadic connection with someone who was loved or hated, or a combination of both. Another set will include the experiences of managing the existence of the third person. For many people these two sets are catalogued as school and home. At school the experiences have to include the passionate relationships of small children and later agonies of adolescents. At home there will also be dyadic relationships and the interruption of mother's total absorption by the presence of father or of the new-born or older sibling. Each of these sets may be affected by the other and the neurotic may be able to rediscover the connections and make more as they tell their story in each area.

One of the criteria for the potential usefulness of talking therapy is the permeability of these areas of experience. In the assessment session, a patient might show a tendency to talk about school experiences more freely than home experiences. Even the occasional question might not be able to divert the flow, and the patient may feel that he does not remember much of what happened at home. In this case there is still the possibility of showing an awareness of the two underlying psychological states. There can be an account of the first girlfriend and included in this experience there can be some hint of tenderness or regret. Even if all that is available to language is not love but just need, and not intimacy but just sexuality, the clinician will be able to detect the sense that there could be more or that it could have been different in some dimly understood way.

Here there may be a difference between men and women or between the mental sets that are represented by biological sex. Culturally, the role of the woman is receptive and nurturing. She is therefore encouraged to look back on her own nurturing as the model and to find good things in what she has received from her mother. She has no cause to be ashamed of the feelings in this set, whether they are the result of a good experience or of the deprivation of what might have been good but was not. A man on the other hand has to deal with the cultural expectation that he will have outgrown his need for nurturing by the time he leaves home to go to school. He is put through a training process which encourages closure of the emotions and the development of a tough exterior which cannot be permeated. Opening up any of the areas of his past experience is bound to be difficult and if the patient perceives the clinician as a mother figure, whatever that might mean in terms of his past experience, he will have to overcome his cultural resistance to making himself vulnerable to her. If the clinician is a man, the patient has to run the risk of his homosexual desires appearing consciously both to him and to his clinician.

Analytic clinicians are trained to think about themselves as potentially either father or mother so that the patient can use whichever aspect of her he needs. The patient will unconsciously respond to the clinician as though she were his father or mother without regard to their actual sex because he is not doing so consciously. The biological sex of the clinician need not define the transference.

Transference is egalitarian. Everyone uses it and knows something about it. Every new relationship is formed on the basis of what we have learnt from the past. The patterns and expectations of the first encounter with a nurturing parent figure may not be remembered, but they are the first members of the set. The initial doorstep encounter with a prospective new patient is equally subject to unconscious processes which may lead to positioning within any of my sets of experience. Robert Hinshelwood (1991: 168–9) gives an illustration of a patient's displacement of his experience from one set to another when describing the predominant transference in an initial interview:

> He spent quite a lot of time going over somewhat repetitively the ins and outs of the work situation. He talked about it in a business-like manner as if presenting a file on a problem at work. The indication is clear; he was presenting himself as if to a manager at work. I appeared before him as the father/employer who might dismiss him and from whom he vainly sought approval.

Seeing and understanding this situation as displacement would be commonplace in the analytic therapies. The more interesting question about such a transference state is that of why it is worth the bother to track it down.

Freud was interested in transference and its effects from the point of view of resistance. He saw the positive effects as important because the patient's love for the clinician helps to overcome resistance. He was aware that the patient's demand for sexual and generally erotic satisfaction can also be a major form of resistance. Freud himself experienced such resistance from Dora and did not recognise that it could be analysed at the time. We are fortunate to be able to learn from his experience. Since Freud wrote his technique paper *Observations on Transference Love* (1915) we have no excuse for not recognising the therapeutic importance, but also the difficulty, of working with the patient's love in all its forms.

Heinrich Racker (1968: 71) wrote: 'The special part to be played by transference in psycho-analytic treatment is to be explained according to Freud by its relation to resistance'. Certainly as a form of resistance to the analytic process, transference is immensely important. The patient described by Hinshelwood (1991) would have had all sorts of reasons for approaching the first meeting with his potential clinician cautiously. He would not be willing to reveal his feelings in undisguised form to a stranger. More importantly he would not be willing to reveal his feelings undisguised to *himself* because the patient arriving for a first session feels particularly vulnerable and in need of protection. He may find that he feels safe enough to reveal his distress, or he may find that he cannot conceal it, but his initial impulse will often be to hide it *if he can*. He is therefore likely to try to prevent himself from feeling it. In this respect the unconscious plays the part of the helpful ally which turns attention and emotion to an apparently safer, more neutral area of experience. Yet because we know that the unconscious, like the small child playing hide and seek, *does* have a need to be found, the clinician is able to find traces of what is hidden in the material that is brought, however irrelevant it may seem.

For this reason, the disguise of feelings by displacement is not the solution that the patient needs. If the feelings were merely disguised, he might leave the session unsure about whether or not he wished to return. The clinician might choose to make a statement about what she understands the transference to be – for example, that the patient is addressing her as if she were a manager at work in the set of father experiences. That still leaves out an essential task. Another process has to take place, the process by which the patient's expectations are understood and rephrased as questions. In all the early encounters, the patient is putting questions to his clinician. Hinshelwood might thus recognise his patient to be asking the question: 'Will you treat me as my manager might or is this something different?'

Hinshelwood's patient might have been particularly concerned with the power of the father/manager to dismiss him or let him stay, and certainly in a first session patients are very concerned about whether they are wanted and whether they *deserve* to stay. Other questions can often be considered under the umbrella question 'What kind of parent can I expect to find here?'

Questions are often a crucial area in the formation of a relationship between patient and clinician. The patient may come knowing that questions are unlikely to be answered. The clinician will have been trained not to ask questions: if you ask questions, all you get are answers. The general prohibition against asking and answering questions has been based on the idea of the *blank screen*. This idea has now been relinquished as impractical (even if it is still seen as desirable), and so the embargo on questions may be re-examined. Sousa *et al.* (2003) have carried out an extensive review of the literature and trace the embargo to Ferenczi (1933) who said that he always tried to answer a question with a 'counter inter-rogation'. Ever since, trainees have learned that the answer to a question is usually another question.

We might re-evaluate the usefulness of sometimes answering the patient's questions. We might also consider that the clinician may ask questions. Sousa *et al.* wish to reinstate the possibility of asking questions from the point of view of recognising the value of the clinician's sense of curiosity. In terms of transference, asking questions will also establish a model in which the patient knows that he is of interest and value. It may also free the patient to ask questions of himself as well as of the clinician: 'Very disturbed patients do not ask. They have become ill through certainty' (Sousa *et al.* 2003: 873). Being able and willing to surprise the patient enables the clinician to establish a situation in which the prevailing trans-ference is destabilised and subject to question.

Because we understand transference to draw its unconscious emotional power from infantile experiences, there is an infinite variety of possible sorts of transference. We would be quite wrong to imply that transference can be categorised. Nevertheless, there are certain positions in which the patient may locate himself which can be recognised by the clinician and may imply areas of need. This is a vital aspect of the transferential relationship and can convey a great deal of valuable information to the clinician, who learns to listen to what she is told and to understand how the messages are constructed.

The process of transference formation is essentially a creation of metaphor or metonymy. Two situations or people who are differ-ent are brought together and made into one. Because the process echoes the creative process of intercourse, it will often lead back to the patient's image of what intercourse is like and this in turn will connect the clinician to an image of the patient's conception and the situation into which he was born. Taking an initial history is standard practice for many analytic clinicians. The initial history will leave much that is unsaid but one of the important areas will be the relationship between the parents. Many of the patients presenting themselves for analytic work at the beginning of the twenty-first century are born to single mothers and have no father that they know.

The emphasis of theory and practice in the twentieth century was very much on the mother–infant dyad and fathers were left to make an occasional guest appearance (e.g. Samuels 1985; Trowell and Etchegoyen 2002). Because we understand transference to draw its force from an unconscious process of creating metaphor, the analyst is constantly presented with the task of interrogating the patient's discourse as if it were a literary text. The great difference is that what is presented to us in a therapeutic session is not a literary text and feels immediate and urgent. Perhaps the therapist struggling with the mixture of emotions and impressions that she derives from the first session will be helped if she can remember that some of this tangle will be unravelled over time when the emotional power from infantile experiences is separated from the images of the present. What makes our profession endlessly fascinating is that there are no cookbooks or handbooks that will make practitioners or our patients safe. All we can offer is the willingness to enter the danger zone with confidence that it can be traversed. The therapist knows that there are fewer traps than the patient thinks. To this extent she must take on the role of the one who knows. What she knows is that patient, benevolent analysis can help. Beyond that she always has to begin at the beginning.

7

THE THERAPEUTIC ALLIANCE: PERHAPS WE CAN WORK TOGETHER

Now that I have considered the immense reservoir of unconscious phenomena that subvert any rational control over even the most cursory human encounters, what meaning can be left for the jargon expression the 'therapeutic alliance'? 'It's obvious,' some would reply. 'How could we work with any patient if there were not a sense in which we are working together in an alliance to achieve something better, some relief of suffering?'

The problem lies in the divided mind, which both enables us to postulate an alliance with one part of the mind and also makes it impossible to believe that there is a clearly definable ego that is not affected by the work of the unconscious. If, as Freud suggested, the patient strives continuously to undermine the therapeutic work, what kind of alliance can there be? Two people meet, both of whom have an area of mind that is unknown to them and both of them have some conscious wish to cooperate. Unfortunately, we often encounter the resistance of the hidden parts and in the darkness of the unknown much conscious goodwill is overruled so that only occasionally can there be a genuine effort to work on a shared task.

A possible conceptualisation might be that there are several forms of therapeutic alliance. There may be an alliance over the nature of the task to be undertaken, although rarely over how it might be achieved. In all cases the conscious version will be subject to subversion by the unconscious. There might be an alliance over how therapy will be attempted. There might be an alliance based on the strength of the affection that develops between the therapist and the patient, a form of benevolence and goodwill. David Malan (1965) uses the concept of rapport and tracks its waxing and waning through sessions as a measure of the effectiveness of his interventions.

A distinction between Eros and Agape might help to express a difference between what is permissible in a therapeutic relationship and what is unacceptable. *Eros* expresses the love that has a libidinal and bodily component. *Agape* is a more general goodwill towards another human being. Psychoanalysis and analytical psychology both show that there may a benevolent and generalised goodwill toward the other without a physical expression. When negative feelings prevail, the memory of some affection may carry the patient through the difficult times. Early responses from the clinician may not be very kind, and in fact may be experienced as the reverse. Times and fees may be set to suit the analyst more than the patient, but if this is done with an acknowledgement of the patient's feelings, the goodwill may become associated even with negative experience. *Agape* might still be an appropriate concept to describe the therapeutic bond.

The humanistic and cognitive therapies set out to enable the patient to work with the analyst to bring about change in areas where change is perceived to be painful and costly. The cognitive therapist will help the patient to observe his own thought processes and when he has observed them to set out to make a conscious effort to change them. The humanistic or person-centred therapist will seek to create a strong, empathetic bond so that the patient will tolerate the lack of guidance. The patient must be willing to accept the effect of the attitude described by Rowan (2001: 11):

> It is clear in Rogers' approach to therapy that the therapist or counsellor may or may not have a great deal of knowledge or experience, but the important thing is to leave it all behind in the actual therapy session with a client . . . This means letting go of knowledge of theory, even of experience of similar cases.

Therapies based on the ideas of Carl Rogers (1965) seek to hand over the leading role to the patient. For this transition to happen, the patient must be willing to face up to a state of unknowing and letting go of certainty. Taoism is associated with person-centred therapies and it places great emphasis on the unfocusing of the mind so that the non-intellectual faculties (feeling, creativity, intuition etc.) can come into play. The mind, in this view, must centre itself on what matters. Rowan gives an example of a potter who worried about making pots with lids that would fit. She was given a beautiful, very old pot whose lid did not fit and she discovered that the fitting was not the important thing. She was then able to centre herself on the essential beauty of the pot. From then on, of course, she had no trouble with making lids that would fit.

The cognitive psychotherapist will give her patient tasks to perform as homework which will usually involve concentrating the mind on aspects of patterns of thought and behaviour. This may be a matter of noting when an unpleasant or conflictual situation arises and registering how one reacts to it. The patient must be willing to experience the unpleasant situation yet again, with no promise that anything will ever feel better. The only way in which such a situation can be bearable for the patient is where there is a strong belief that the therapist has a plan which will lead in the end to improvement. In other words, there is trust in the wisdom and therapeutic skill of the clinician.

Freud was interested in the relationship between patient and analyst, but because he discovered the importance of transference, he spent most of his energy on identifying positive and negative transference and their effects. His advice on beginning the treatment was recognition in some measure of the importance of the way in which the analyst sets up a climate in which free association may be more or less possible. Sandor Ferenczi (1933), however, devoted his attention much more to the question of how the personality, action and behaviour of the analyst will affect the response of the patient. He was concerned with the effect of the reality of the analyst on the positive or negative transference, rather than seeing the transference as given only by the patient's experience. Separating transference from the agreement that the patient makes with the analyst was one route to the concept of an alliance. Elisabeth Zetzel (1956) referred to the *treatment alliance* by which she meant to imply that there was an area of the patient's mind that would retain the trust that the analyst would work with him and for him, however angry with her he might become.

This belief would be of great comfort to psychoanalysis but unfortunately raises some difficulties. When it is encountered in the analytic process, resistance often seems to leave little of the mind of the patient to be an ally. How are we to distinguish between the rational judgement of the patient that, for example, the work is not being helpful enough to him and the resistance of the sick part of the patient? In the Middle Ages, exorcism was intended to deal with precisely this problem. The devil was invited to speak and was expected to object strongly before he would emerge from the patient, shouting and swearing his protest. This clear distinction between the patient and the resistance may have helped to keep some poor women from being burned as witches. Psychological practitioners have less reliable methods of distinguishing the patient from the illness. Robert Hinshelwood (1997), seeking to untangle the question of how we can claim that we can ever have informed consent from the patient, does not even attempt to follow this line of thought. Instead, he develops the response to a different question: what can the patient be consenting to? He gives an illustration of a patient apparently consenting to what he was offering:

> The patient consciously thought very highly of me and my interpretations. She continued to come but contrary to expectations my interpretations rarely moved her. They did not touch feelings that were problematic for her. She always agreed with me and thought about all that I had said. Often she would start one session by recapping where we had got to in a previous one. There was an intellectual quality about it. When I pointed out such processes she agreed pleasantly.
>
> (1997: 90)

This patient began to speak about work colleagues who got on with their own work but did not cooperate with her. Hinshelwood was then able to begin to hear and express her anxiety about 'getting cooperation going'. When he spoke about this, she accepted the interpretation but was still not moved by it. She was however able to apply it in a 'chatty way' to what was going on with her colleagues at work. Freud's criterion for judging an interpretation by the associations that it brings would not have helped much in this context. The material that followed seemed to show that the interpretation did have an effect, but the analyst could see that the effect was being carefully controlled.

Hinshelwood was then forced into the position that we must all take up eventually. He began to look at the meaning of his experience of her admiration of him and what was being demanded of him in the transference. He concluded that it was the transference of a narcissistic parent–child relationship of mutual admiration. He was to admire her but not change her, and it was to this (and only this) that she was giving her consent.

If this were all that could be said, we would have to face a difficult ethical question. What right have we to proceed with treatment when the clinician is thinking something very different from the patient about the purpose of that treatment? However, Hinshelwood goes on to describe a dream that the patient reports in which some men come and push her car out of the way when it is parked in front of a shop. Hinshelwood is able to see in this the re-entry of her own worries about herself. In the purely narcissistic child–parent required relationship she would do nothing other than be a pleasing child and would leave him to do all the worrying. Both in making this interpretation and in its content, he is demonstrating a hypothesis that there is more to her desire than the surface wish for admiration. He is working with the assumption that every clinician has to make, which is that we have a better understanding of what the patient wants than the patient can have when they first come to us and ask us for help. Part of the help that we are trained to give is our persistence with our informed view of what the patient really needs as opposed to what the patient feels they need.

How can we tell whether we are right in this sort of situation? Hinshelwood tells us that his patient's response when he told her what he thought she was telling him in her dream was 'I hate those sorts of interpretations'. Because this was a different sort of response from the previous chatty and easy ones, he was convinced that he had reached something of importance and that it had some sort of truth. He then goes on to consider psychoanalytic paternalism which is shorthand for the attitude that 'the therapist knows best'. He mentions the rules for medical consent in which the patient gives prior consent to an operation which will be carried out while he is unconscious. If the surgeon encounters some unexpected problem, he will have to deal with it as best he can because it will not be possible to wake the patient and ask him to give additional consent to a different procedure or to something which could not have been foreseen. In the same way, we might argue that the patient gives prior consent by coming to psychotherapy sessions and, like the skilled anaesthetist, we will gradually enable the patient to regain consciousness after which we will be able to discuss the rest of the treatment with the now more wide-awake patient. This leads to the paradox that meaningful consent to the psychoanalytic process, which involves some understanding of the power of the unconscious, cannot be obtained until *after* psychoanalysis has enabled the patient to know from first hand experience that he has an active unconscious.

Sadly, this argument has flaws. Winston Smith in George Orwell's *Nineteen Eighty Four* does not consent to his treatment, of course, but he comes to love Big Brother as a result of it. The fact that the patient at the end of analysis assents to its premises and agrees that the treatment has taught him the power of the unconscious might not be either a persuasive or an ethically acceptable argument.

Hinshelwood examines some other arguments that might allow us to relax over the issue of consent, none of which is satisfactory. Even the patient's option of walking out is not a tenable guarantee of consent while he is there. We know only too well that patients are held in their analysis by infantile and unconscious ties which the analysis itself needs to dissolve. These ties might be very different from the rational consent that is implied by the term 'informed'. In the same way, walking out may be either an expression of resistance against an abusive or inappropriate treatment or it may be an expression of unconscious and infantile patterns of experience and behaviour which need to be analysed so that they will not interfere with the patient's emotional life in the future. Walking out might be a dangerous event rather than a positive expression of rational choice although, of course, sometimes it may be just that. All too often patients are connected to damaging or useless therapies by a self-destructive bond which makes walking out next to impossible. The patient also hopes that the therapy will be repaired eventually and will also repair other old wounds that have seemed irreparable. Clinicians have the responsibility of preventing such therapies from beginning or at least helping them to end.

When a treatment continues for some time and is meeting with some success, the patient may be better able to integrate some parts of himself that had before been unconscious. Hinshelwood's patient, Miss C., dreams of the men who push and damage her car. They seem to represent the unwelcome appearance of something that she does not wish to recognise. The task for the analysis is then to find a way in which she can recognise what this disowned part of herself might mean to her and to see whether she can find herself stronger for having pushy men than for being the pleasing, narcissistic person that she had apparently been before. In Jungian terms she would be finding and recognising her shadow:

> Consideration of the analytic situation leads us to the conclusion that we have a conscious component and an unconscious component in the therapeutic alliance as in any relationship. We have no justification for separating a conscious and rational treatment alliance from an

agreement which is continually contaminated and changed by its unconscious components. We cannot separate conscious from unconscious in this way and there is no easy way out of the dilemma.

(Hinshelwood 1997: 98)

The theory of attachment helps to show what elements of the opening sessions will be important in forming an attachment to the therapist that can be used: 'Attachment is more than the re-establishment of security after a dysregulating experience and a stressful negative state; it is also the interactive amplification of positive affect states as in play states' (Schore 2003: 34). Schore goes on to add that the establishment of a secure relationship enables the development of a 'positively charged curiosity'. This is a state in the infant but it must also be a prerequisite for uncovering psychotherapy in which curiosity must outweigh anxiety about what will be discovered. Many clinicians working intuitively have tried to create an environment which minimises accidental happenings that can arouse anxiety while leaving open some of the anxiety that arises from gaining access to the unconscious. Whether or not this state of readiness is possible is a matter for the clinician to consider before taking the patient into therapy. The patient's task is to assent at an unconscious level. His assent must inevitably form part of the treatment alliance but not the conscious part. We can also take some encouragement from Schore's statement that affect regulation is not just a matter of dampening negative emotion, although we recognise that useful work is unlikely to be done in an atmosphere of prolonged negativity, but also involves 'an intensification of positive emotion' (Schore 2003: 34).

Such findings from attachment research limit the usefulness of the view that in practice the treatment alliance is the agreement that is formed at the assessment consultation Both parties are aware of the conscious agreement that has been made but the clinician is aware that much more is needed from the patient than his conscious consent. The patient has said what he hopes for and the practitioner has undertaken to work with him. Ethically, the clinician is bound to work for the patient's well-being and that is about as much as the patient is likely to be granted in the way of a guarantee. The exact method of treatment cannot be delineated before the work begins. All that the psychoanalytic practitioner can offer is that she will say whatever she can to help to elucidate what the patient brings. The obligation to make a trial interpretation is therefore not only a matter of assessment so that the therapist can see whether the patient can use what she is offering, it is also an ethical imperative in that it enables the patient to feel the power of the psychoanalytic method and to come to some conclusion about whether he wishes to submit himself to the emotional demands of the consulting room. This is also an argument for making the assessment as much as possible like the ongoing work.

Many therapists have argued that the opening session has all sorts of special excuses to be different. Questions may be asked to an extent that would not be contemplated in ongoing work. Taking a history requires that the narrative should be filled in, although there may be noticeable and interesting gaps. If, for example, the patient does not mention his father, the therapist will note the omission but might well then ask what part his father played in his early life. Sexual history will usually be taken and very often comes only as the response to specific questions.

Another school of thought favours the completely open assessment in which the therapist gives no guidance to the patient, who is simply provided with a comfortable chair and a waiting listener and tells his story as he thinks fit. This latter approach might be more useful to the patient who is better able to give consent to the treatment if he has already experienced the silent listener who merely waits and will not dictate an agenda or gratify the infantile wish for reassurance that the listener wishes to hear. The unconscious is called upon to give its assent to the treatment since the conscious mind has very little to enable its complicity.

There have been and still are methods of treatment with even more complex ethical difficulties. Jay Haley (1976), for example, developed the technique of the *paradoxical instruction*. This was carefully kept within ethical boundaries but nevertheless caused some unease because it worked entirely without the conscious cooperation of the patient.

Haley worked with a boy of 9 who masturbated in school, in front of his mother and sisters etc. Haley emphasises that he defined the treatment goals clearly as ending the public masturbation, not masturbation altogether. He worked with the boy by setting him a programme in which he would masturbate on Sundays (when he had said that he enjoyed it most) twice as many times as in the previous week. He was to do it the prescribed number of times even if he had to get up early to get it done. Haley describes the way the therapist deals with the boy's response until the behaviour is extinguished. Similar techniques could be used with adults and the point is that the therapist uses his knowledge of his own authority and the likely response of the patient to that authority. There is of course an alliance and that is to the treatment goals at the beginning which have to be agreed at some level between patient and therapist. The boy of 9 was quite capable of assenting to a treatment plan that involved stopping the obsessive behaviour that got him into trouble because the therapist emphasised that he was to continue with the masturbation that gave him pleasure in private, on Sundays.

This view of the alliance as being formed before treatment begins, based on the broad agreement that the patient wants to feel better, is probably what most practitioners rely on to validate their activities. There is still a problem for analytical therapists in that they will usually interpret the withdrawal of consent as resistance and will not change their approach or agree to the patient ending. In most cases the patient withdraws consent by simply refusing to attend sessions.

We may not be able to prevent this problem from arising but we might be able to be more helpful in the same way as doctors are when they warn about physical pain or the risks that may arise from a proposed treatment. We can make it very clear at the beginning that the treatment is likely to be painful. We also have a duty to point out that there are other forms of treatment from which to choose. For example, in the case of severe depression, all responsible therapists would consider whether an assessment for medication could help the patient and could perhaps enable the patient to make better use of psychological therapy. There is an argument that some patients are too depressed to benefit from psychological therapy and must be treated with anti-depressants to prevent what might in the worst cases end in suicide.

This discussion implies an acceptance of the role of external reality. The therapist presents some aspect of her perception of the possible reality for the patient of the proposed treatment and the patient is expected to answer with the best of the conscious, thinking mind that he can muster. We probably have to accept that this is as close to informed consent as we can get. The therapist for her part is obliged to take into account the changing and unreliable nature of the patient's perception as well as the way in which the process of the treatment in itself is bound to make a difference, whether for better or worse, to the patient's ability to tolerate the treatment and its demands.

The pre-treatment agreement cannot be taken as the whole story. Both the patient and the therapist may need to revise their view of what the treatment involves. In other words, the formulation of the presenting problem is only as good as the patient's self-awareness and ability to recognise his own problem can make it. The therapist will have to take account of the patient's expressed wishes but will also have her own way of formulating the direction that she thinks the treatment needs to move. If the therapist is not willing to work towards the goals expressed in the presenting problem, there is an ethical problem in taking on such a patient. For example, a patient who comes expressing a self-centred attitude, complaining that everyone else is selfish and that she always has to do all the work, might be asking for help in getting other people to do more for her. The therapist's private view might be that the patient needs to discover that she need not demand so much from others and could consider offering more rather than less herself. In such a case, the therapist might need to say that she would work towards helping the patient to form more satisfying relationships. Modification of the patient's formulation would be more honest and could encompass both the therapist's and the patient's view of what is needed.

If the patient is willing to subscribe to the new formulation, the therapist can assume that there is a treatment alliance even though the way in which the treatment proceeds will probably involve the therapist working to develop the minority part of the patient and will involve undermining the patient's conscious attitude to himself and to others.

So far, I have emphasised the unconscious component of the treatment alliance. The work of the ego psychologists centred on the need for the ego to perform its function of relating to external reality. In reaction to the Kleinian view that the only useful interpretations are those that identify transference, the ego psychologists opened up the possibility of using other sorts of intervention which, following the lead given by James Strachey (1934) in his paper on mutative interpretations set out to show the patient how he was departing from a perception of the reality seen by the analyst. Strachey thought that the most important element of the transference that would need to be analysed would be the functioning of the superego. If the primitive superego were unmediated by an experience with a tolerant and loving parent, the primitive, harsh superego would be projected onto the analyst and the difference between the projection and the reality would form the material for interpretation.

Of course, Strachey understood that the curative effect of recognising the gap between the transference perception and the reality would take place only when the patient himself could see the difference. Interpretation might at first have no apparent effect at all. In Strachey's view, there is a cumulative effect of pointing out that the patient's perception is not borne out by the analyst's behaviour. If the analyst says, 'You seem to be afraid that I disapprove of what you have just said,' the patient may deny that he was afraid but, if the analyst has caught a genuine moment of anxiety accurately, the patient may begin to consider that the analyst's willingness to speak about it might imply that there is no need to be afraid. The patient may come to understand that the perception of discomfort is unnecessary because the analyst might not be the cruel and demanding superego figure that was lurking in the emotional response, although not consciously perceived.

Can the patient identify a positive side of the analyst? If so, there is a possibility that he can identify constructively with it and later, in Klein's terms, introject it. The formation of a split in the ego between its observing and participating functions is an important part of the ability of the patient to make use of the therapeutic work. Such a split is a necessary part of any change. It is necessary for the analyst as well as for the patient to be able to separate these functions, participating fully in what is happening in the session at one moment and then being able to stop and think about what is happening and what the effect has been. The patient's ability to do this may not be very conscious or deliberate but must develop if he is to be able to make use of the experience of the therapeutic relationship. Elisabeth Zetzel (1956) used the term *therapeutic alliance* to emphasise that the alliance is essential for change, and the main quality that is required is the willingness to trust the analyst.

Founding the therapeutic alliance on the ability to trust the analyst is obviously appealing to those who are interested in developmental concepts. Psychologists such as Erikson (1965) have shown the importance of trust to the young baby. Attachment theory has followed the idea that the infant can form attachments only when there is an ability to trust. Secure attachment to the analyst may be seen as a condition for emotional development and growth and this is so from the most infantile fixations to the more mature ego states that patients strive so hard to achieve.

Psychoanalysts have an interest in every aspect of human development from the moment of conception to the moment of death. Willingness to think in interdisciplinary terms means that we can now have some meaningful idea of a preconception history of the individual and of the metaphorical impact of the individual's experience of his own ability to conceive. The therapeutic relationship will have to have its moment at which the sperm and the egg make contact. Symbolically, the sperm of the penetrative partner in the relationship must be able to penetrate the egg and make a conception which will lead somewhere:

> Under the influence of love making that is geared to reproduction even a hitherto egalitarian couple often become sexually polarised. The partners may begin unconsciously to live out their image of an inactive ovum passively awaiting impregnation by the fittest piercing sperm in the sexual fantasy of their male and female bodies coming together.
>
> (Raphael Leff 2003: 39)

Raphael Leff is here pointing out one form of imagery that might apply to the beginning of a relationship. Intercourse that may lead to the conception of a baby may provide an image of the possibility of fruitful work in therapy, although the prominent image in the twentieth century was that of the mother and feeding baby.

Whether or not we accept the relevance of the image of conception, we could hardly fail to acknowledge that there are differing images of passivity and activity and that these may make a match or a standoff. If the therapist believes that the patient must speak and make the agenda from the very beginning of the first session and the patient also sees himself as the passive, receptive partner in the couple, the therapist is likely to fail in the sense that there will be nothing but an absence and a fruitless wait for the active sperm that neither partner is producing. The novel *Inconceivable* by Ben Elton (2000) charts with painful humour the experience of the man and the woman in a couple who are 'trying' for a baby. The sadness of converting lovemaking into a campaign in which the chances of conception must be maximised before all else is brought out in the novel perhaps more clearly than in Haynes and Miller (2003).

Trying is what goes on if both partners desire therapeutic success. Without some sort of trying there is unlikely to be any success. Yet, trying in itself can be a blight on spontaneity and joy. Elton's couple demonstrate the fruitlessness of too much trying, and John Klauber is saying something of the same sort in his paper on spontaneity in interpretation. He argues that 'the spontaneous processes are responsible for the artistic and most creative aspects of the analysis'. He advocates using not only logical thought but also spontaneous thoughts in communication: 'it is the spontaneous communication of a new idea that evokes a spontaneous reaction in a patient' (Klauber *et al.* 1987: 33).

A therapeutic relationship needs to have the quality of potential. The patient will wonder about the potential of the analytic relationship but may ultimately have to face the reality of barrenness or a low level of excitement if that is his experience. The possibility of a trusting relationship based on a perception of the real nature of the analyst is not acceptable to all schools of thought. The Kleinians for example are not easily convinced that there can be a relationship that is not a part of transference and therefore subject to all the distortions of transference. If the therapeutic alliance is conceived as being different from transference in that it has some privileged accuracy, then it is difficult to accept. Nevertheless, the young baby has different emotional states, in some of which we might recognise that negative transference of hate and fear predominates, but there are also other states in which the dominant emotion is neither idealisation nor persecution but a trusting expectancy in which something new could be allowed to happen.

A satisfactory way of conceptualising alliance could be by simply hypothesising a split between the transference perceptions and the ability to form an underlying working alliance based on trust and the positive experiences of the analyst. This is not, however, theoretically acceptable to a Kleinian who would see all perceptions of the other as being based on transference rather than a hypothetical reality. The danger of promoting a positive alliance that is distinct from transference might lie in missing the negative transference while basking in a positive valuation of the analyst. This positive valuation might reach the level of idealisation which would be less likely to be overlooked, but it might also lead to a comfortable collusion which might be problematic in that it could be a reason for maintaining the status quo rather than enabling the disturbance of analysis. Safran and Muran (2000: 9) point out that an emphasis on the therapeutic alliance can lead to an over-valuation of the rational conscious processes at the expense of the unconscious.

A further danger is the risk of collusion which would lead to a comfortable alliance between the patient and the analyst and a failure to probe beneath the surface. This is known to analytic therapists as a *transference cure* and implies that the transference itself remains untouched. The patient may feel better temporarily but the distinguishing mark of a transference cure is that it does not go deep enough to last. The alliance that has been made and used is between two unreal structures in the analyst and the patient and therefore cannot lead to anything of lasting value.

The first area of alliance that many psychotherapists might wish to be able to accept is the possibility of agreement over the nature of the problem and the intention of the therapy or analysis to remove it. Such a view of a therapeutic alliance is fraught with difficulty. Hinshelwood's cogent case, showing just why it is that we cannot believe in any such alliance also shows the difficulty in arriving at an agreement over the direction that the treatment needs to take (Hinshelwood 1997). First of all the patient is coming because of a fault, flaw, misconception in his psyche; probably many such faults. By definition therefore the patient is not in a position to join with the therapist in a definition of what he needs on any basis other than compliance with the desire of the therapist. The patient most often comes asking for the removal of a symptom, but the analytic therapist cannot wholeheartedly agree with this as the aim of the treatment. She may agree that the patient's life would perhaps be better if he were not functioning in such an obsessive, phobic, hysterical or perverse way. She is, however, bound by theoretical constraints to be interested in the symptom as communication and cannot therefore join in a wholehearted effort to get rid of it until it has been understood in full speech. She will see it as embodying some value for the patient which must not be lost, at any rate until its purpose is put into words at the symbolic level.

The patient is not even in a position to know what his goals need to be in terms of achievements or changes in behaviour. In this, analytic practitioners are in a very different position from the person-centred followers of Carl Rogers. Rogers holds as a canon of his belief that the patient knows what he needs even if he is blocking and preventing himself from recognising it. Therapists of both models might be able to agree that the analytic work is to find out what the patient needs, although the routes taken will be different. The analyst seeks to find the voice of the Other who hides behind the conscious busyness over jobs, relationships, ambition, everyday life. She takes it as her role to catch the slips of the tongue, the images in dreams and fantasies and to help the Other to find a voice in this way. The person-centred therapist believes that all she needs to seek to do is to free the patient from the bonds of anxiety and distrust that hold him back from connecting to his own self: 'People are all right as they are' (Rowan 2001: 36).

As a representative of person-centred therapy, Rowan (2001) has only two references to *transference* and none at all to *therapeutic alliance*. He says of transference that the analytically trained psychotherapist would use it as a major tool but the person-centred therapist would 'merely pay attention to it and use it as necessary'. (2001: 114) This makes the use of transference sound rather easy. A complication for the analytic psychotherapist is that she is aware of working all the time within a transference and therefore the aims that may emerge as a shared alliance with the patient will emerge from within the dominant transference at the time. Once again, Jacques Lacan (1966) has something useful to say about the alienation of desire. Each person needs to discover what has happened to the flow of his desire: is he still enmeshed in the toils of his mother's desire that he should function as her phallus? The process of analysis helps the patient to discover whether what he takes to be his desire and his intention in entering therapy is in fact his or someone else's. One of the most important aspects of the achievements of therapy is that the person will change his view of who is speaking for him and who else is implicated in the tortuous path that his thoughts have taken. The person speaking at the beginning will often strongly urge the initial desire, whatever that is: 'I need to be more confident', perhaps. The clinician will ask: 'Who is this with whom I am being invited to align myself?'

Hinshelwood (1997) gives an example of alienated desire. A university student comes for analysis saying that he cannot sleep and therefore might fail his exams. His conscious wish is to be able to find out what stops him from sleeping and change it so that he can sleep and then of course pass his exams. Any analyst or psychotherapist worth her salt will immediately be asking whether this student might have a conflict with his own desire. The Other in him does not wish him to pass his exams. Why not? Taking the alienation of desire as an important concept, one might ask, who does not wish him to pass his exams? This sounds at one level like a fairly simplistic counselling matter. Find out what you really, really want and go for it. There could be a perfectly satisfactory therapeutic alliance based on this quest. Both analyst and patient might well agree that it sounds like a reasonable basis on which to proceed. Yet we are still going to be tripped up by the 'beauty behind the shutters' who will agree with a course of action only to sabotage it. We come back again to the difficulty and wonderful opportunity provided by the knowledge that there is no such thing as a straightforward alliance between two psyches, since both are at the mercy of the Other.

The second arena for a therapeutic alliance is the way in which the aims of the analysis are to be achieved. In this, almost every other model of psychotherapy is at an advantage over the analytic. The cognitive behavioural therapist can say very clearly what her treatment plan will be. She can set out the rationale and the steps by which a particular problem will be approached and overcome. The patient may or may not accept and acquiesce but he knows what he will be doing and if we are correct in postulating the interference of his own unconscious, the patient and therapist can proceed on the basis of an alliance to defeat its efforts to resist. The humanistic psychotherapist will be perfectly clear that she is seeking to free the individual to be himself. This will be done by increasing trust through the core conditions of empathy, genuineness and respect so that challenge can become possible.

The analyst on the other hand has no such clarity. She may also wish to say that she seeks to free the patient from certain bonds that are holding him back but she will be hard put to say exactly how. Most patients are satisfied with an honest statement that the treatment cannot be described in advance because it will be different for everybody. We can say that we will listen and observe and say something when we are ready, but that is hardly a very detailed treatment plan and a patient might well complain that there is not much possibility of forming an alliance with such an unsatisfactory and partially formed intention.

Can we then conclude that we can form an alliance with the healthy part of the ego that brings the patient to analysis? Hinshelwood is convinced that there is a possibility of forming an alliance of some sort: 'It is the adult in the patient that the psychoanalyst will address when he speaks' (1997: 135). Nevertheless, he is not ignoring the infant in the adult. Donald Winnicott (1960), for example, discerned elements in the psyche that he called the true and false self. In this model, the false self brings the true self to analysis. In the initial session, the false self sits in the chair and speaks to the analyst while the true self remains hidden, waiting to be found. Lacan was inspired by some of Winnicott's ideas and was influential in that he saw the analyst's task as liberating the true self when the false self could allow it to appear through gaps in the conscious discourse. Lacan emphasised that the true self is unconscious and will have to be actively sought out.

He pointed out that there is a danger of analysing the false self because it complies with the therapy and like an anxious parent will say 'Yes doctor, whatever you say, doctor.'

Lacan defined transference as a phenomenon in which both the analyst and the patient are involved as the subject. This is a single subject: the unconscious. It is the only appropriate subject for psychoanalysis. Transference for Lacan is a matter of experiences that come through language:

> The efficacious transference which we're considering is quite simply the speech act. Each time a man speaks to another in an authentic and full manner, there is in a true sense transference, symbolic transference – which changes the nature of the two beings present.
>
> (Lacan 1954: 109)

This view precludes the possibility of any relationship of value outside the transference because it is within the transference that the important symbolic changes take place. Repetitions of behaviour and reminiscence of memories may be part of this approach to symbolic or full speech. If we can never get beyond the transference in which both parties are enmeshed, perhaps we can be content with speech acts and our attempts to make contact between the complexities of the combined unconscious process of two people. At least we can both be united in being less sure of what was once held to be certain but must remain for ever in question.

8

COUNTERTRANSFERENCE:
LOVE AT FIRST SIGHT

Countertransference is a term that first made its appearance in the 1950s. Freud had found that his work was subverted by transference. Working out those problems left him little time for a theory of countertransference. Because the clinician must experience the early therapeutic state in an inchoate and often confusing mixture of affect and intellectual response, the theory of countertransference has often seemed like a good reason to push the confusion back to the patient. The new-born clinician is subject to a buzzing, brightly lit chaos of impressions and of course seizes on theory or neurotic defence to make it bearable.

Implicit in this statement is the understanding that the practitioner is also a subject and an object to her own unconscious. If the patient sees through a filter tinted by his past, so does she. Few would now argue with the importance of recognising, as James Rose (2000: 454) points out, that the encounter in the consulting room is always a 'meeting of two minds'. Rose quotes Goldberg: 'The fluidity of the exchange of information in messages between patient and therapist does not allow one to isolate either the one or the other as a fixed point in order to gain access to some reliable set of mental contents' (Goldberg 1998: 215).

Since subjectivity is more than simply an absence of objectivity, there is a difficulty in arriving at a view of what the meeting of two minds can be. For John Rowan and the humanistic school the central concept is dialogic:

> The whole idea of a dialogic relationship is relatively new and entirely valid and important. Where I think its proponents go wrong is when they somehow think they have

to give up the idea of a central self in order to preserve the idea of dialogue. I am not quite sure why this is.

(Rowan 2001: 81)

Beyond the idea of dialogue is the idea that we are constricted from an essentially social being-with-others and that we are inevitably formed by our connections with others: 'In other words the way that we play sports, the way that we talk to each other, the way that we relate to our children are all grounded in a socially constructed nexus of meanings and interpretations that are not of our making' (Cooper 2003: 19). In twentieth-century philosophy and in the humanistic therapies we find agreement that the human subject is constructed socially and therefore the therapeutic process will return in some way to the dialogue which seeks to understand the nature of the structure. The therapist will use herself in this and needs to be available from the very first moments to reflect on the effect that the patient has on her and no less on the effect that she is having on the patient.

We still have to deal with the question of truth. Can I ever say that I am right and the patient is wrong? Freud believed that the psychoanalyst would be protected from making errors by her own analysis, which would have taught her how to hear the reverberations of her own psyche and distinguish them from those of the patient. We have much experience since then to lead us to believe that the training analysis can do much but it cannot render anyone immune to the effects of their own unconscious.

The Lacanians pursue the question of what is meant by intersubjectivity further than other schools, for whom it might be merely an acknowledgement that there are two unconscious processes in the room. Palomera (1997: 144) sees a way through the impasse that this could create:

Lacan affirms in Seminar 1 that feelings are always reciprocal. To say to a patient 'you think I am angry with you' or 'you believe that you have seduced me' necessarily converts the analyst into a subject that desires, that is to say, identical to his enunciation. From which follows the well founded reply 'You're the one who says it'. However, by trusting the feelings rather than the word that determines them, psychoanalysts came to trust their own feelings as the place of the manifestation of a truth repressed in the Others as indisputable testimony of unconscious knowledge. The problem is, as we have just seen, that the reciprocal is equally true.

The analyst in this way becomes the locus of the speech that comes from the Other who is both the unconscious of the patient and the unconscious of the analyst. This view can be valid only if the analyst is allowing herself to listen and to be connected to her patient. Palomera adds 'He who listens is heard to speak'. He also considers the argument of the Kleinians that the practitioner internalises the psyche of her patient in order to speak from it and then projects it again. Lacan believed that it was the ultimate failure of this process that would lead to the end of the analysis, when the analyst is no longer the spokesperson for the patient's unconscious.

Historically, the idea that the patient's transference would have a useful effect on the analyst if it were to be considered as communication at the unconscious level, arose during the twentieth century. Freud had, however, laid a foundation stone for a strong and tall structure by discovering that the patient's projections surviving from the past could be useful, although they might also remain the problem that they had first seemed. The idea that the patient's transference is perceived through specially attuned systems in the analyst developed later. Paula Heimann (1950: 81) proposed the thesis that 'The analyst's countertransference is an instrument of research into the patient's unconscious'. The idea that the practitioner's response to the patient could be taken as information from the patient is attractive and has won broad acceptance except among the French school. David Livingston Smith (1991: 51) argues against the validity of both transference and countertransference because both require the belief that the analyst can separate her own responses from those of the patient:

> Taken together these factors conspired to justify an analytic stance of virtual omniscience and an immunity to the sort of disciplined self criticism that is essential to the growth of any real science. Far from being as Freud described it, the last great blow to human narcissism, psychoanalysis has become a bastion of grandiosity.

This useful critique does not mean that we need to dismiss the usefulness of countertransference. Rather it implies that we must pay attention to the patient's unconscious communication as a commentary on the therapeutic relationship in the present. This is already a possibility in the theory as it was developed by Heimann (1950) because she was proposing that the therapist should use the countertransference as an instrument of research, not as an excuse to blame the patient for all that was painful. The emphasis in recent practice is much more on the openness of the practitioner to the patient's questions, fears and anxieties as they are directed to her with or without the overt influence of the past.

Heinrich Racker (1968: 105), in his thorough exploration of transference and countertransference, was still defining counter-transference as having a twofold nature:

> First it may help, distort or hinder the process of understanding the unconscious processes. This effect relates to the analyst's role as interpreter. Secondly the patient's transference will have an effect on the analyst and he will have a response of some sort to it.

Racker considered that the patient's transference would be liable to promote neurotic reactions which might hinder the analyst's ability to perceive the patient's process (1968: 105). In both of these senses countertransference is always present just as is transference. Like transference it is rooted in the Oedipal situation and will derive its unconscious energy from the power of the Oedipal residues of the analyst. The patient will represent an Oedipal object for the analyst, as Harold Searles (1959) points out. He identified three consequences of this Oedipal discourse:

- The analyst will react to and eventually renounce the patient as her love object.
- The parent normally reciprocates the child's Oedipal love with more intensity than has generally been recognised. This aspect will have strong implications for the therapeutic relationship.
- Thirdly, the passing of this stage of Oedipal development is important in ego development as well as for superego development (1959: 284).

Searles acknowledged that, with all the patients he saw for inten-sive psychotherapy or psychoanalysis, he experienced feelings similar to those that he had experienced towards the end of his own analysis. These were romantic and erotic feelings, which expressed various longings for the patient. Initially he reacted to those feelings with anxiety and guilt, fearing that he was particularly prone to exploiting his patients for help in resolving his own unresolved Oedipal wishes. Countertransference was still not widely seen as a concept through which a clinician could come to understand these feelingss. Searles gradually came to see them as informative in that they indicated the need for the analyst to progress through Oedipal tensions with each patient. He finally reached the conclusion that the countertransference, just as much as the transference, must be resolved by the end of the analysis.

Most of the writing that has followed from Searles' ideas has emphasised the need for changes in the analyst. The assumptions and judgements that are a part of anyone's transference to a new individual must be recognised by the analyst so that there can be a genuine understanding of the other, something that in the terms of Martin Buber ([1923] 1958) would be considered an I-thou rather than an I-it experience. This is of course a dangerous process. The analyst will need to recognise that she is attracted to some patients and repelled by others. She may even suffer the temporary psychosis known as 'falling in love'.

There is of course no question that the patient must be allowed to discover and integrate his sexual self. The clinician is responsible for what should happen if her own feelings are strong enough to prevent her from working and if she feels that she cannot hide them and manage them in herself. Just like the parent who finds his or her child sexually desirable, she must be able to enjoy the attractiveness but not react to it. If she knows that she cannot do this, she must end the therapy and refer the patient to someone else. This is best done at the very beginning when the referral will need no more explanation than simply, 'I don't think that I'm the best therapist for you. I shall recommend places where you might look for another therapist.'

Feelings of attraction at the beginning may be misperceived as a response to a potentially successful working relationship. If the feelings of attraction do not emerge until later, the question of how to renounce the love object is much more difficult and may become in itself an excuse to do nothing. The therapist may well think that she will do more harm by ending the therapy abruptly than by continuing. Of course she will be tempted by any argument to enable her to keep her Oedipal love object. For this very reason, all reputable regulatory bodies make clear that a sexual relationship with a patient is absolutely forbidden. Unfortunately, an emotional relationship that is tinged with sexual attraction is much more difficult to legislate. This is an area in which the profession might well be divided about where therapeutic good ends and harm begins.

Gerard (1999) argues that the patient needs to be loved by the therapist at some point. This will be in response to knowing something of the patient and his struggles and is not the initial feeling for him. Therapies that work on the basis of repairing deficits rather than revealing conflicts will perhaps be more inclined to allow and even encourage the therapist to demonstrate affection for the patient as long as it is not sexual. Keeping this line clear is one of the great difficulties for the therapist who allows touch. If, from the beginning, the patient's wishes to be held, hugged or caressed by the therapist are gratified, how will he manage the deprivation of finding that there is a point beyond which she will not go? Certainly this is the problem of the parent, who will normally hug and kiss his child but must be clear that this is not a preliminary to anything more. This sort of restraint might well be a useful piece of learning for the patient, but it must be based on an absolute clarity in the therapist that there are no circumstances in which she will alter her firm boundaries.

Hunter and Struve (1998) argue that although there is a dearth of research on the effects of using touch in therapy, there are arguments for its use within the constraints that they carefully define as ethical. They note that the refusal to touch will evoke images of parental refusals and affectional deficits that the patient has experienced. This they propose, along with other arguments, as a good reason to touch the patient. The counter argument is that this effect of deprivation in the therapy can be interpreted verbally and will lead to the patient learning to deal with deprivation rather than relaxing into gratification which will be very difficult to end (1998: 102). What must be recognised is that the deprivation applies to the therapist as well as to the patient, and although the demand may not arise at the very beginning, the therapist faced with an impasse may well wish to offer some non-verbal comfort as a way of feeling that she is doing *something*.

By the time that the therapy ends, the process will have brought about changes, first to the analyst and then to the patient (Gerard 1999; Murdin 2000). The analyst must change through the process of understanding her own internal state and seeing that the patient plays a part that connects with her own past as well as his. She must recognise her transference to him and that she is implicated in the therapeutic drama. She must see that she designates for the patient a part in the dialogue that commences the first moment that she agrees to meet a potential new patient. She must then have the humility to extricate herself from the scenario that develops and by doing so she can model for the patient the way in which he can extricate himself also from the painful dramas that he sets going with each new encounter. Psychotherapy has a moral component. Peter Lomas (1987: 135) is not entirely alone in his unhappiness that psychotherapists 'believe that they are not concerned with how people should live but with helping their confused and abortive attempts to live the kind of life that they choose to live; that they are beyond the concerns of how one ought to live'.

Staying out of value judgements is difficult, but the profession becomes very dangerous if one subscribes to the view that therapists should get involved with how their patients ought to live. In the area of countertransference, however, no one can evade moral choices and some consideration of how to live well.

Mr F. seeks therapy because he is having terrible arguments with his fiancée. She wants to get married but he is not sure that he is ready for marriage and wants to put it off. His whole family urge him to get married and think that she is a very nice girl. She would be welcomed as a daughter-in-law, sister-in-law and so on. He comes to see Mrs X., an analytic psychotherapist whose husband died some ten years before. She finds herself feeling very impatient with Mr F. She would like to say to him, 'Just get on with it, don't be such a wimp.' Her impatience rises to such a point that she can no longer frame useful interventions and she seeks consultation. She describes a session in which Mr F. speaks about his terror when his girlfriend speaks of her ideal of marriage as a state in which she will be protected and safe. 'What about me?' he asks. 'Who is going to make me feel safe?' The therapist had replied, 'Perhaps she wants to achieve a situation in which you can feel that you have the power and the strength for both of you.' Her colleague then asks how Mrs X. is managing as a widow. She thinks about this and discovers that she still feels very unsafe and somewhere has developed a phantasy in which Mr F. is going to look after both of them in the therapy. She thought at the outset that he was very intelligent and perceptive and would be able to do the work for himself. She would simply sit with him, like a wife in the passenger seat, and enjoy his ability to do the driving for both of them.

Once she had seen the scenario into which she had inserted herself, Mrs X. was able to begin thinking differently. The next time that Mr F. began to complain about his fiancée's demands, she said, 'I think that you have been experiencing me as being like your fiancée in that I have been waiting for you to be strong enough to find the solutions that you need. You are I think needing a more mutual endeavour to discover what you need. You do not wish any longer to be the baby who is helpless and simply waits for mother to come and relieve all his distress. On the other hand, you cannot be expected to carry all burdens on your own.'

While this interpretation was not immediately transformative, its effect in the long term was to show that Mrs X. was not willing to allow everything to stay as it had begun. The phantasy, in which Mr F. was going to replace the man she had lost, had to be abandoned and in its place Mrs X. had to accept the less desirable reality. She might not have been totally correct in saying that she thought Mr F. did not want to be a helpless baby. Most people want to be a helpless baby at least some of the time, but she was correct in her judgement that he might be better able to judge that for himself than if she further infantilised him by making such a statement. In making a careful interpretation which took account of the patient's need to be recognised as an adult by his therapist, she was beginning a relationship in which both people could be prepared to acknowledge a need for help from the other.

I am concerned here with the effect of the patient on the therapist at the outset of psychotherapy. What difference will it make to a therapy if the analyst either is or is not attracted to the patient at the outset? Arguments from the Rogerian school of person-centred therapists as well as from analytic therapists such as Gerard propose that the patient who is not able to inspire some love in his therapist by the time the therapy ends is in need of more therapy: 'I think it is only when a patient can arouse our deepest loving feelings (not empathy) that we can really hope for a truly positive outcome from our work' (Gerard 1999: 29).

Gerard says that in her own therapy she urgently wished to know whether she was loveable and that led to a need to know whether

her analyst loved her. I would guess that most of us who have experienced analytic therapy would be able to recognise that need. Gerard's analyst is quoted as having said, 'When you come to feel loved by me then you will know.' This was a response that she was able to use and it led her to the conclusion that all patients need to acquire the conviction that they are loveable. However, she does add that 'I hope I have not conveyed that love is all that is necessary to a psychotherapeutic relationship' (1999: 40). She would also consider interpretation and interventions to be vitally important while recognising that there are times when interpretations will feel persecutory and times when they are entirely what is needed.

While agreeing to some extent with Gerard's point, I would like to emphasise that the analyst is likely to be looking for the reassurance that she is loveable also. Perhaps those who choose this profession are particularly susceptible to the need for this kind of conviction to be reinforced. A patient arrives in the consulting room of someone who is in need of further assurance. The patient may well be angry, hostile or suspicious. The analyst will begin by accepting these feelings. Anyone with a responsible training would expect such negative responses. On the surface, then, we are mostly quite capable of accepting the negativity of the patient who says, 'What are your qualifications? Have you the necessary experience to deal with me?' These questions may be asked overtly or through unconsciously designed material. They are likely to be disturbing because they will imply a fear of a basic incapacity in the analyst to provide what the patient needs. Someone who is competent will be confident enough not to find these questions disconcerting. Others may well react in a way that closes down the therapeutic relationship.

A patient went to see a well established and experienced analyst. The patient had been to a psychotherapist before and was used to a fairly open approach. She therefore asked the analyst, 'Do you have supervision?' He was immensely offended or at least appeared to be so and said, 'I do not consider that I need supervision at my level of experience.' The patient, who was not in a very stable state, said, 'Well I think that is irresponsible and I shall not choose to work with you.'

Such a scenario does of course ask questions of the analyst's narcissism. We might hope that we have all been through a sufficiently rigorous analysis to understand something of our own needs and vulnerability. Nevertheless, Nina Coltart (1996: 32) agrees with Neville Symington, who suggested that a psycho-analytic training would increase rather than decrease narcissism: 'A long personal analysis, which we all have as part of our training, leaves the narcissism stronger and the ego weaker than they were at the beginning of analysis. This is a condensed comment and a significant one and it repays a lot of careful thought'.

Careful thought about the analyst's narcissism has to leave the therapist with the opinion that we are very susceptible to the temptation to satisfy narcissistic needs through seeing patients. This will perhaps be one of the unconscious elements in assessment of potential patients. Very often the analyst's need is for a patient who will allow a successful analysis and this will of course coincide with the patient's need. We can have some confidence that we will all be doing the best that we can to achieve this, but the judgement about what route should be followed to lead to that outcome has to be that of the clinician. Patients are not in a position to know what treatment they need and how the clinician should proceed. This is obviously an element in consulting any professional, although most other professionals, such as medical doctors or lawyers, can give a clear and useful summary of the approach that they intend to take.

More dubious results of the professional narcissism of the analyst may arise from the need for an Oedipal love object. The effect of this need will show itself in different ways with each analyst and each patient. The patient described above who asked about supervision is arousing the analyst's omnipotent need to be able to function without help from anyone. He seems to have felt a need for the patient to be willing to accept him as the authority who is so powerful and so benign that no further restraint or limitation on his supreme power is needed. He is undoubtedly experienced and much of the time his work will be impeccable, but he is apparently determined to receive homage from his patients that will reinforce his confidence in his own ability. Parents of course do this to their children and in some cases the child will be accepted and shown love in proportion to his willingness to gratify the parent.

Few analysts would be so grossly unaware of their responsibility as not to notice a patient who is excessively compliant. On the other hand, many patients have learned throughout their lives to be subtly pleasing to the person that they are with. The first session will give the patient an opportunity to begin to discover what the analyst desires. For example, the well attuned patient will soon realise that the analyst does not want apparent compliance. This is a challenge to create 'compliant non-compliance'. Other patients will be only too pleased to bring negative transference. Some may know the term and may have sufficient sophistication in psycho-analytic terminology to be aware of what they are offering. Others will discover that the practitioner is keen on displays of anger or attacks. In such cases the less intensively trained counsellor is most likely to be saying in effect, 'It's OK to be angry.' Of course it is *not* OK for anyone to be angry. It is a painful, dangerous and destructive emotion and those who invoke it willingly are exposing themselves to some difficult work for which they may not be well equipped.

If the patient is actually angry but afraid to acknowledge it, there may be good reason for seeking anger out. If the patient is angry with the therapist, there may not be much doubt about it and the therapist may be consciously aware of spoken words of anger or of behaviour on a spectrum that runs from the subtlety of a banged door to the retaliatory refusal to attend at the times on offer. On the other hand, we are all aware that some forms of anger are repressed, not available to the patient, and show themselves only in a silence which is uncomfortable and has an element of fear in it. Anger may show in apparently innocent behaviour such as missing sessions for perfectly good external reasons but which leaves the therapist feeling that something is being left unsaid and that something might be hostile.

Therapists deal with the suspicion that anger is lurking beneath the surface in various ways. Some may be perfectly at ease with it and have no problem in convincing the patient that the anger exists and can be owned. Others find this much more difficult and are likely to seek to mitigate it in various ways by placating the patient regarding whatever they think is causing the anger in the present relationship. In this situation, some therapists will be particularly keen on clinical concepts such as the *therapeutic alliance*. Karen Maroda (1991: 2) puts the case against using this concept as a means of escape. She states the view of some of the faint-hearted:

> The rough idea being that there was an innocent suffering patient who was more or less at odds with his demonic psychopathology . . . The obvious weakness in this for-mulation is that it never really permits the integration of

the whole person . . . The easy way out is to say I care
about him but hate his pathology.

The emphasis here is on the therapist's defensive use of clinical
concepts against the powerful feelings which come not from some
demonic part of the otherwise delightful patient, but from the
whole energy of the person who has reason to be angry. Maroda
points out the relatively obvious truth that patients, no matter how
sick, may well be able to observe the therapist and arrive at some
perfectly justifiable conclusions. In fact, the more disturbed the
client, the more likely his antennae are to be able to pick up the
minutest shades of feeling and response in the therapist. Such a
patient may well at times become angry with his therapist and she
may need to search her conscience not only for the theoretical
library but also for the thought or feeling that might with justification have made the patient angry.

Jacques Lacan did not evince much enthusiasm for the
possibility that countertransference might be anything other than
the analyst's transference to the patient:

> Actually if the analysand can be the cause of desire in the
> analyst, if a passion is eventually stirred up, one might ask
> whether those feelings when passed through an analysis
> are equivalent to those which the analyst himself produced
> . . . it is nothing more than a case of transference.
>
> (Palomera 1997: 142)

Such a conclusion detracts from any special value that might be
given to the countertransference as conveying something special
about the analysand. In fact, Palomera says that it merely leads to
the question of who is in analysis with whom. Even if that were the
sum total of its use, we might still hesitate to throw it away. Each
analyst needs to work all the time to analyse her own transference
to the patient and to make sure that it does not blind her to the
material and affects that are being brought. Some writers enthusiastically embrace the value of using the practitioner's own feeling
response with the patient and this may well be helpful as long as it
has been carefully sifted by someone with experience of thorough
personal analytic work.

What interested Lacan about countertransference was the
attempt of the analyst to fill the gap that is always being revealed
in the structure of the patient that is in turn revealed to the analyst.

The gap that Lacan is showing is the absence of the signifier of the analyst, based on the idea that the analyst is the one who is *supposed to know*. This is a position that must remain empty unless the analyst is sufficiently grandiose to try and take it. Lacan's conclusion is that we are dealing with a single subject, that of the unconscious, and both analyst and patient are implicated. He gives to the structure of the transference the power to transform both the analyst and the patient.

To return to the beginning of the relationship, the patient, on first arriving at any session, is bound to evoke an emotional response in his analyst even if it is nothing more than boredom. Jeremy Holmes (1995: 35) writes of the affective relationship in terms of attachment styles: 'As the interview progressed I began to feel an almost physical sensation of grappling with this powerful man as if I were wrestling'. Racker (1968) dismisses these initial struggles as neurotic in the analyst. The task of any therapist is to deal with the events in herself and not to inflict anything on the patient unless it is appropriate to do so. However, Maroda (1991) argues that the therapist's emotional response is of great value and in fact the therapy will suffer if it is not used and often openly revealed to the patient. One effect of an attitude which encourages the open expression of countertransference feelings is that the resistance that they encompass on the part of the analyst will have to be overcome to some extent. A therapist who is willing to do this is at least not ascribing all the pathology or all the madness to the patient. But how much of the inner thoughts and feelings of the therapist can be usefully expressed in the first session? At this stage the patient is largely unknown and the therapist must learn through trial and experiment how responses will be used.

Maroda (1991: 110) argues that the patient is in any case aware of the response of the therapist and therefore an acknowledgement will be reassuring and will be felt as a sign that such feelings are not to be feared:

> There are three basic reasons for revealing the counter-transference. The first is that the patient is aware of his therapist's feelings and he suffers from the distortions and confusions that arise when his therapist denies or circum-vents his reactions to the patient. The second reason is that the patient's opportunities for delineating, understanding and taking responsibility for his own motivations and behaviour are limited by the therapist's refusal to do the

same. And third, to the extent that the countertransference is not resolved within the treatment relationship it can lead to an outcome characterised by countertransference domination in which the past of the therapist is repeated and determines the course of treatment.

This third point is an important indication of the way in which a person's therapy can be dominated by the neurotic needs of the clinician. There is no reason why we would not expect to find therapy being used for the resolution of the therapist's issues, and this does often happen and may be one of the reasons why people are willing to stay in a profession which is emotionally demanding, highly stressful and financially often unrewarding. If the therapy of the therapist is a byproduct of the work that needs to be done for the patient, no one would object; but if the therapy is hijacked from the beginning by the therapist's repetitions, that may well inhibit the patient and swamp his own need to repeat his experience and his opportunity for the replay which might be essential for his own return to greater health.

In order to safeguard the use of disclosure of the therapist's response, Maroda indicates that it should be done only in response to a specific question about it from the patient. In the early stages of treatment, she asserts that patients will rarely if ever be ready for analysis of the dynamics of transference and countertransference. The patient will be asking for disclosure *only*. Most patients will be seeking unconsciously, or occasionally consciously, to provoke a countertransference reaction but the purpose of this is to enable the needed repetitions to take place. Thus a patient may need his clinician to replay the over-anxious or intrusive mother. Very often, the analyst will recognise the pressure that is coming from the patient and will be able to analyse it. Analysis of the dynamics might not be usefully disclosed at the beginning. A patient will be likely to interpret any comment about intentionality on his part as an attack.

A history of aggression in the patient might be a contra-indication for inexperienced therapists. Any prospective patient who describes physically attacking or even being tempted to attack someone is not suitable to be seen by an inexperienced therapist or anyone working in isolation. An experienced therapist on the other hand might decide to rely on her experience of the patient. If he does not frighten her, she may decide that the story of aggression is a show, to hide his fear about a lack of potency. She may decide that she can deal with his fear and will take the risk that if he begins to get better he may begin to be more able to carry out his hostile wishes. If he can understand his fear he may acquire the potency that he needs without so much aggression.

On the other hand, the patient who arouses fear in the experienced therapist is conveying a message, at the level of unconscious to unconscious, that he cannot trust himself. The wise therapist will decide not to work with such a patient for both their sakes unless she is well protected, preferably within an agency and not on her own. The Hopi Indians say, 'Run towards your fear'; this cannot often apply here because the therapist is not the only one who would have to be willing to confront that fear. The patient is likely to be even more afraid than she is, and if any work is to be done she must take responsibility for ensuring that she is safe. Both people need to be confident so that the fear may be safely addressed.

A second fear in the therapist that needs attention is caused by psychosis. The psychotic patient is unlikely to come without any history and most will tell the therapist, if asked, whether or not they have a psychiatric history. Yet there is a particular kind of icy but apparently causeless terror that may occur only momentarily but deserves very careful attention. Sometimes this fear is accompanied by bodily symptoms. For example, a woman suffering from severe paranoia that was usually under fairly good control sweated excessively and filled the room with the smell of fear. A therapist with such a patient might guess that the challenge would be great, probably straining her willingness to go to the edge of the precipices in the patient's mind. To work with such a degree of disturbance, a therapist needs good support and confidence in her own sanity because it will certainly be shaken.

On the other hand, mildly neurotic patients are often capable of arousing maternal feelings in their clinicians. Maroda (1991) urges us to consider whether it would be possible to say 'I find myself wanting to take care of you' in the very early stages of an analytic treatment. She does however reveal that her intention is to convey an atmosphere in which self-revelation becomes acceptable and is in fact the nature of the expected discourse. She emphasises that the patient often asks questions of the analyst at the beginning, such as:

- Do you have any children?
- Are you married? or
- Are you a Christian?

These are questions intended not only to extract an answer but also to establish the parameters of the relationship. Maroda takes the unusual step of offering to make a deal in which essentially one says to the patient: 'I will show you mine if you show me yours'. She is enthusiastic in supporting this approach and says that patients in her experience accept the deal with enthusiasm. She also points out that the logical corollary of her argument is that oppositional behaviour will lead to oppositional effects and this will be familiar to the more conventional therapist. If you simply analyse a question or ask what the answer would mean to the patient, the response of the patient comes out of humiliation. The traditional analytic attitude would regard this as a necessary process which can be understood and used. Patients need to learn that therapists will speak when they are ready and cannot be compelled to answer.

At the first session, there will often be feelings and experiences, for both patient and therapist, which may be obvious and easily named but may also be subtler and more difficult to label. The patient will expect to have all sorts of experiences in the first session in response to the therapist. Some of them will be an expected reaction to a demand or a desire which the therapist may be making consciously or unconsciously. The therapist will equally be responding to the patient and of course, according to her training and theoretical model, will be hearing the demands and desires of the patient. For most analytical therapists, there is a layer of understanding which will be reached only through the unconscious.

One of the most frequent comments of assessors running initial interviews and writing reports is that there is 'something else, something that I am not sure about that is going on beneath the surface'. Therapists have well developed antennae and when there is something of this undercover sort going on they are likely to understand it as a communication which is being blocked at source. The most useful assessors will leave it at that. There is something else which cannot yet be defined or put into words and the receiving therapist will have to work to discover and verbalise this unknown something. Other assessors will strain anxiously to unravel what has become a challenging mystery, trying to verbalise their hypotheses prematurely. They may turn out to be right or may be leading the ongoing therapist off on a wild-goose chase.

In either case, the theoretical importance of countertransference is being recognised. There is nevertheless a debate to be held over the extent to which countertransference is a valid or useful concept. Lacan (1951) not only challenged the existence of a separate category of experience to be called *countertransference* but was also unconvinced of its usefulness, since he designated it as a resistance on the part of the analyst. It is the 'sum of the prejudices, passions, perplexities and even the insufficient information of the analyst at a certain moment of the dialectical process of the treatment' (1951: 225). By defining it in such a way, Lacan made it clear that the analyst cannot use such feelings. She must be willing and able to delineate them and then put them aside. In this way Lacan returned to a position closer to that of Freud than that of Klein.

In the initial session, there is plenty of scope for resistance on the part of the analyst. Because two people are meeting for the first time, differences will be acute and there are plenty of occasions for prejudices to be felt and either given some space or repressed. Repression of course does not mean that they are without effect, only that they are removed from the range of thoughts that can receive conscious attention. Few analysts are likely to entertain the idea that they might have a prejudiced response to the more obvious forms of difference such as race, culture, class or sexual orientation, but they are *not* immune. Responses that are repressed will be more dangerous, and, as Lacan says, will form the analyst's resistance to the work of analysis.

We have therefore to consider that the useful definition of countertransference is the therapist's response to the transference that the patient brings to the therapeutic relationship.

Clinicians report an infinite variety of responses to patients and some would ascribe the whole of their response to *projective identification*. For most people however, the initial sessions are a time to begin a process of disentanglement of me from you, which is one of the main tasks of the analytic therapies. The beginning shows the extent of the task and the clinician is the one who must begin immediately to recognise the size and complexity of what is undertaken. Ascribing the emotional tone of the encounter immediately to one or the other is not helpful. The whole of a therapy which may last for years will still not have made the limits of the self totally clear, since psychic space is not the same as physical space, but if a therapy is worth having it should be able to convince both parties that the task is ongoing and can always be tackled and taken a bit further.

9

WHAT DO I DO NOW? THE BIRTH OF THE PROFESSIONAL SELF

In this chapter I shall discuss the beginning of analytic training. How do the initial incentives to begin this work affect the kind of therapist who emerges? At the beginning of the twenty-first century in the UK, the training of analytical therapists is based on a hierarchical system that has no obvious relationship to merit, aptitude, outcomes or practice. Nevertheless, the location of the training will have a powerful effect on the work that the candidate will be likely to undertake and may in some cases preclude certain areas of work, particularly in the UK's National Health Service.

The three main areas of training overlap to such an extent that no one can satisfactorily define what makes them different. They are currently defined only by the decision of the training organisation to assign its graduates to a particular place in the hierarchy. The most satisfactory rationale for the levels of training and practice is based on the intensity of the work represented by an index of the frequency of the sessions offered to patients. The area of once-weekly work is the preserve of counsellors, who are rarely encouraged to see people more often than this. As far as I know, no counselling training actually gives experience of more frequent work. Psychotherapy occupies the middle ground of twice and three times weekly work. It bears some resemblance to the state of the middle classes: well educated and cultured but aware of not being at the top level. Psychoanalysis occupies the position of the aristocracy. In 2001, the Institute of Psychoanalysis defended its monopoly of training in the UK against a challenge from psychoanalytic psychotherapists and has refused to allow any other organisation to impinge upon its hegemony. It currently holds firmly to its self-proclaimed right to be the only organisation that can hand down the pure gold of psychoanalysis to others.

How do people come to each of these layers of training and why do they begin where they do? I suspect that few people ever ask themselves which level they would prefer to enter. I have the impression, that like class in Britain and elsewhere, one is 'born into it' and most will remain where they first find themselves, although a few decide that they see no good reason not to improve themselves and move up to the next level. One of the major influences in choosing a particular training or in choosing to train at all comes from one's own therapy or analysis. Identification with the therapist is powerful and may contribute to the healing process; in a number of cases it leads to a career choice or a career change. If the patient is vulnerable because he or she is in a process of change both internally and externally, seeking to find what will make a satisfying life, then it would not be surprising if looking at the one who sits in the seat of power, the one who is identified with the parental images of creativity and wholeness, leads to a desire to have what she has.

Of course, if the therapy is any good, the therapist will question this desire in order to discover how much substance there is in the wish and how much it is a magical or omnipotent expectation that the patient can have the life of the therapist for himself. In spite of the questioning, the major reason given when applicants for training are interviewed is they were helped by therapy and would like to offer something similar to other people. This motivation must be interrogated. A desire to save the world is one of the most dangerous motivations because it leads to omnipotent, charismatic therapy and is often at the root of decisions to break ethical boundaries. The therapist with such a motive is likely to think that he or she knows what the patient needs and knows better than anyone else. 'What the patient needs' may in these cases look to the therapist like sex or friendship, but is less likely to be the hard work for which only a thorough training is adequate preparation.

There are of course other reasons for finding oneself in a particular kind of training. Outside London and the major cities in the UK there are very few psychoanalysts and not many psycho-analytic psychotherapists. For that reason we would expect that most people would be trained as counsellors. Certainly the numbers completing training confirm that this is so. The British Association of Counselling and Psychotherapy has about 20,000 members. Membership is not related to any standard of training and many are not actually trained as counsellors. The UKCP has about 6000 registrants, all of whom are qualified psychotherapists.

Since counselling is a profession with much larger numbers, we might reasonably expect to find more counsellors, both in employment and in work with individuals. Yet this is not the major route into counselling training. In many positions, counsellors work with specific client groups and with specified tasks such as bereavement or adjustment to illness such as cancer or AIDS. Difficulties at work provide another major area for counselling. Clients presenting with these problems are likely to finish their often time-limited counselling and leave, in order to get on with their working lives. By contrast, like psychoanalysts, most psychotherapists, across the theoretical and technical models, are working with patients who have less specific needs and who are likely to take some years to complete their work. In such cases, after the most immediate problems have begun to lose their urgency, there is time for the patient to reflect on his progress and on the role of the healer that is evident in front of him, and decide that he would like to train as a psychotherapist or psychoanalyst.

What happens next? The applicant approaches a particular organisation and finds out what is required. If it is the organisation where her therapist trained and is therefore one of the established psychotherapy training organisations, it is likely to require personal therapy. The humanistic and person-centred models of psychotherapy have different views of what is needed for training. They require evidence of personal development but are happy that this can be acquired through, for example, a personal development group rather than individual therapy. The demand from the analytic training for individual personal therapy with an approved therapist is thought by many to be essential for that model, but in the area of counselling it is still controversial. As we move along the spectrum from generic counselling to psychodynamic counselling we find a greater emphasis on the need for personal therapy. Not everyone accepts the necessity and some counselling courses merely ask for a specific number of sessions such as 20 or 40. It is difficult to see what can be achieved by such a short period of therapy for the practitioner who wishes to work with her own clients for as long as is needed. Of course, many trainees will decide that they need more therapy once they have experienced the power of the analytic method.

There are still some trainees who object to being asked to have therapy. They might well be asked why they wish to preach and not practise. Presumably the person who believes that she does not need her own therapy believes that she is already able to access her own unconscious. Such a stance conveys a fundamental misunderstanding of the difficulty of the project. Freud carried out his own self-analysis, and most people would acknowledge his exceptional willingness to examine his own weaknesses, and yet he still found areas that he could not access. He concluded that the analyst is able to see and hear some things that the patient is bound to miss. Becoming a patient is also a test of the would-be therapist's willingness to be vulnerable and her understanding of the value of accepting the help of another.

I can therefore adduce various arguments for the necessity to have personal therapy in analytic training. One argument in its favour is that the would-be therapist needs to know what it feels like to be a patient. For the psychoanalytic practitioner, there is a much more important question which may lead to an answer as to why we cannot accept that personal therapy is unnecessary. How can you teach psychoanalysis? The answer for Freud was that you teach it mainly through a training analysis. The old methods of training in the Institute of Psychoanalysis involved the training analyst as the judge who would declare that his candidate was ready to undertake training and in particular would be ready to take on a training patient of his own. Finally, the training analyst would decide when the analysand was ready to qualify. The analysis thus acquired two different agendas, one of which was to prepare the candidate for the future practice of analysis, handing down by modelling the technique and even in some cases the theory of psychoanalysis to the next generation. The second agenda was the one which for other patients is always the first: the relief of suffering and the freeing of the ego from its subservience to unnecessary neurotic defences.

This dilemma did not go unnoticed but until very recently it was regarded as an inevitable problem. In psychotherapy, some training has managed to allow the candidates to have their analysis for themselves while hoping that they would be learning useful and ethical patterns of behaviour. In this model, the analyst will not be asked for a view when the organisation is selecting the candidates for training. This abstention makes the process of selection more difficult. Mistakes will be made. Because selection is still subjective, the selectors can be taken in by false-self structures and by the applicant's passionate desire to train. There will be painful situations in which either the candidate or the training organisation has to decide that this person will not make a sufficiently helpful or ethical practitioner. We are of course very fortunate if we discover this before the training begins. A recent unpublished research project (Schumeli 2003) showed that there is a correlation between the attachment style of the interviewer and the attachment style of successful candidates. Using the Adult Attachment Interview, this study drew some interesting conclusions about the process of selection but does not indicate how we can improve it in order to be more confident that we are selecting the most suitable candidates. It does perhaps imply that we must ensure a variety of attachment styles in our interviewers. We now need some further research to indicate the correlation that exists, if any, between attachment style and outcomes in the work of therapists.

While we do usually learn about the mistakes that we make in selecting therapists, we are unlikely to know about the mistakes we make in the other direction. There are the potentially excellent therapists who have been turned down and have either gone else-where or have taken up other work and abandoned the idea of working in the talking therapies. Would we perhaps do better if we were to ask for the opinion of the training therapist about the suitability of the candidate. Some organisations have until recently made this the principal method of selection but most are re-evaluating the desirability of this practice and have decided to withdraw from this position. The disadvantages of leaving the therapy uncontaminated by such a judgement are outweighed by the value of the therapy to the candidate, who will be more likely to feel sufficiently safe to reveal his or her doubts and weaknesses. We can hope for better therapists in the long run if we agree that a lifelong search for self-knowledge is a necessary condition for training.

Since training courses require that analysis begins and con-tinues for some considerable time before the first training patient is taken on, the first day in training will be supported by the analyst who has already experienced this frightening moment. I remember the first words that were spoken to me as I contem-plated the coffee and biscuits set out for us newcomers. Another newcomer said, 'You look pretty miserable. Cheer up. It may never happen.' At the time I was grateful for being able to speak to someone. Her breezy desire to help and make things all right caused difficulties for her with the analytic model. After the first year she disappeared and we were never sure whether she left of her own accord or was asked to leave. I, on the other hand, had to face my shyness and reserve and to discover an ability to speak in a group.

In the days when I trained, most of the teaching consisted of setting a series of psychoanalytic papers to be read each week. The analyst who was in charge of psychopathology would sit and wait for us to speak. She shuffled through some papers trying to find the one that she had set for that day but never showed any interest in the paper and never actually spoke about it. Sometimes, if she felt expansive, she would tell us about a patient that the discussion brought to her mind. We certainly benefited from her experience and her clinical wisdom but we learned nothing of the theory that we could not between us elicit from the papers. That may be fine and may be all that training should be. After all, there is no cookbook for therapists. We all have to face the pain of not knowing what to do or how to help. Nevertheless, I believe that this particular method of teaching meant that it took me years to acquire the necessary understanding of basic theory so that I could relate ideas to each other and critique ideas from a position of knowledge.

Candidates in a pluralistic training appreciate Klein: 'Klein's ideas always excite interest. Whatever one thinks of her style of writing her ideas burst from the page with vigour' Linda Buckingham (1994: 298) writes of the experience of teaching Klein to first-year trainees. She describes getting lost on her way to a seminar so that she was 15 minutes late and was greeted by some hostility. She used this experience later in the seminar to relate the ambivalence of the trainee group when faced by her late arrival to Kleinian ideas about the introjection of the bad object (1994: 302). In the ten weeks of her seminars, she says that there was a process of assimilation by which, in about week five, those participants with the more disturbed patients were beginning to be able to see that Klein's description of the paranoid fears of the infant is helpful in working with such people. I certainly *liked* Klein. There were concepts which I could grasp fairly easily and which had clear relevance to the clinical situation.

John Hill (1993) describes his relation to Kleinian theory and the way in which he found his way to a Kleinian analyst. For him, the interest in Klein came before he found his analyst; there emerged a sense that Kleinian analyses refreshed those parts that other analyses did not reach. Little of content was divulged but there was a discernible atmosphere, rather like Hilaire Belloc's assertion that Balliol men possessed a 'tranquil consciousness of effortless superiority' (Hill 1993: 464).

Hill also illustrates the learning process by which the analyst may influence the candidate but only within certain limits. He began with a Kleinian, Charles Anderson, and although he had no previous experience of analysis he felt that there was something wrong with this analysis:

> Finishing times bore only a broad relation to starting times and sometimes the sessions lasted over the fifty minutes but more usually were truncated. One evening session ended when his wife knocked on the consulting room door to say that dinner was ready . . . He also felt free to answer the telephone and to have quite long conversations with callers during the sessions.
>
> (1993: 465)

When Hill voiced his disquiet to Anderson about these practices, he was told that he was obsessional and that his analyst was not. Clearly, Hill was not happy with these practices and would not imitate them himself. However, he went next to Esther Bick whose timekeeping and boundaries were immaculate: 'All sessions started and ended exactly on time, a practice that I adopted as an analyst and have continued ever since' (1993: 466).

Hill's paper represents a critique of the theory that he was learning as well as of the boundaries of his first analysis. Most candidates in training are extremely anxious, at least in the early stages. In this, they have much in common with their patients. They may be open enough to self-observation to discover how much of the patient's experience is known to them already through their own initiation, but they will have all the confusion caused by a training supervisor and by their teachers who may well have views that are different from those of their training therapist.

The training course will have to provide both for those who are relatively new to the concepts of analytic work and those who have already been in therapy or analysis for some time. Each course will need to work out how it teaches fundamental concepts and ethical issues. Any training has the first duty to ensure that its trainee therapists do no harm. Second, it must ensure that they learn to carry out the best practice of which they are capable. The burden of this will be shared between the elements of the training: analysis, teaching and supervision.

A group of new candidates in training has some excellent opportunities for practical learning about psychoanalytic theory.

The new arrival soon discovers that there is a hierarchy. Some of the sense of who is where on this ladder will depend on the level of experience. Each person watches and listens and forms a view of the others. One has been a community psychiatric nurse or a psychiatrist and has much experience of mental health patients. Another seeks to command respect through stories about his important role as chief executive in a large company. These previous roles may bear little relation to the actual clinical ability or the previous knowledge of the theory, but this will emerge gradually. Another major area of distress for the new trainee is the competition over analysts and therapists. Just as there is a hierarchy in the profession as a whole, so there is a hierarchy among those who are obtaining their therapy from the members of the three classes.

Juliet Mitchell (2003), in her study of the importance of sibling relationships, points out that siblings who share the same mother are more likely to know each other and to support each other than those who share the same father, but may never know each other at all. She argues that the birth of a sibling is a crisis of annihilation. The new sibling will teach the older one that his or her uniqueness is wiped out. There is now another who is able to attract and win the attention of mother and father. A group of new trainees inevitably constellates the anxiety of this potential annihilation. One thing that is known for certain at the beginning is that everyone is a sibling in the sense that there is a parental couple comprising the training analyst and the training organisation. If it should happen that two members of the group share the same parent then the sibling rivalry will become intense and will be very difficult as it may lead to feeling that the one place of safety that had been experienced before is now invaded and spoilt by the unwanted sibling.

Even if the training organisation manages to ensure that the members of any cohort do not share the same analyst, there is no question that all share the same parent in the organisation itself. However assessment is to be done, there will eventually have to be some judgement made about who is ready to graduate and when. All the offspring are required to learn and embrace the ethos of the training whatever it may be. For example, there are some organisations that remain very authoritarian, handing down decrees which are not explained or negotiated. Others have moved to the democratic and consensual end of the spectrum and require the candidate to come to his or her own decision about readiness for independent practice. If this is the case, the training group usually holds the veto and is able to convince a member that the group will not endorse readiness. The authority and the law therefore resides somewhere outside the individual even though the extent to which individuals take responsibility for themselves varies considerably.

There are many ways in which the beginning of training can be spoilt. The Oedipal situation that is set up with the analyst and the organisation may be modified or diluted by the arrival of the training supervisor on the scene. In counselling training this is often a group supervision in which, once again, the candidate faces his or her Oedipal difficulties in allowing siblings to take their turn and have their share of approval. Within the boundaries set by a confident and experienced supervisor, this rivalry may be constructive, fruitful and remain friendly. If the supervisor has not dealt with his or her own narcissism then they will be too concerned with their own image in the group to be able to help the trainees deal with their problems. Difficulties within the supervision group can be extremely painful because it is the place where useful work must continue for the sake of the clients and yet the time must allow for some attention to the needs of the distressed older sibling who cannot tolerate the existence of the other.

Supervision is troubled not only by the feelings of the siblings but also by the arbitrary nature of the way in which the supervisor may be allocated to each group. Unless we are able to pay attention to attachment styles and cognitive styles, we are unlikely to be able to avoid the kind of problems that arise when a trainee says something like, 'I cannot learn from this supervisor – she is too silent, too intrusive, too demanding.' There are infinite reasons why particular people will not be able to manage this relationship. If the beginning were the beginning of therapy, the trainee might just decide to move on and have an initial meeting with someone else. In supervision this is not possible.

Styles of supervising and beginning the supervisory contract vary between supervisors and this initial meeting may make a considerable difference to the rest of the work. Some tasks must be undertaken in the first meeting. The supervisor needs to know something of the background and experience of each person. He or she will wish to set out the parameters for the supervision. For example, everyone needs to know what kind of presentation will be required. Some supervisors are happy with a general discussion and in any case may wish to be popular and avoid making great demands of their trainees. Nevertheless, there is much to be said for asking for a verbatim account of one session with each client once they have been given a general introduction. This will be difficult but will allow the supervisor to track closely the ebb and flow of the session and also to hear the exact words of the counsellor. How else will they be able to help the counsellor to work more effectively?

The supervisor will also have to set the scene at the beginning for the ethical requirements of the training supervision. The specific ethical and clinical accountability for each patient and for the work of the trainee will usually be clear to the supervisor but also needs to be made clear to the trainees from the outset. Permission to speak about the patient must be given in writing by the agency for whom the work is being done. The confidentiality of the arrangement is often taken for granted but supervisors may wish to check that the patient is being told that the confidentiality is limited and that supervision does take place. The supervisor will also have to consider the relevance of the UK Data Protection Acts of 1984 and 1998 for this work. If notes are taken, the supervisor will need to decide how they will be filed and how much detail will be included. They will also have to decide how the notes will be identified or coded. At this point the supervisor may also make an arrangement to be responsible for client contact in the event of the supervisee's illness or death. If they do not wish to do this, they may prefer each supervisee to find their own professional executors or check that the agency for which they work is willing to take this responsibility.

Whether boys or girls, men or women, patients come to a psychoanalyst, psychotherapist or counsellor to discover or rediscover a self to live in. Of course we are not constructing something from nothing and our first task is to survey the building materials, the foundations and the attempts that have already been made to mount a useful structure. The self needs the ability to speak to others in order to make connections with them. It also needs a history to place it in a social and cultural context and to enable a belief in the continuity of the generations and the generative process. The early states to be discovered through the necessary procedures of beginning therapy enable us to see how the patient may be able to move on to use his ability to communicate, to negotiate, to take account of the Other of his unconscious and the other in the room. To begin with he may show us only what is stopping him from moving. Gradually we hope that the movements required by the relentless rhythm of the sessions and the passing of the weeks and months will bring about change.

We might aim for the compression and cogency of poetry, but few of us can achieve it often. T. S. Eliot (1942: 208) understood the process well:

> We shall not cease from exploration
> And the end of all our exploring
> Will be to arrive where we started
> And know the place for the first time.

REFERENCES

Alvarez, A. (1992) *Live Company*. London: Routledge.

American Psychiatric Association (2000) *Diagnostic and Statistical Manual IV (DSM IV)*. New York: American Psychiatric Association.

Appignanesi, L. (2000) *The Sanctuary*. Toronto: McArthur & Co.

Asper-Brugisser, K. (1983) Five reflections on a beginning of analysis, *Journal of Analytical Psychology*, 38: 111.

Attwood, T. (1998) *Asperger's Syndrome*. London: Jessica Kingsley.

Barr, A. H. (1946) *Picasso: Fifty Years of his Art*. New York: The Arts Press.

Bass, E. and Davis, L. (1988) *The Courage to Heal*. New York: Harper & Row.

Bateson, G. (1979) *Mind and Nature*. Toronto: Bantam Books.

Beutel, M. and Rousting, M. (2002) Long term treatments form the point of view of the former patients, in M. Leuzinger-Bohleber and M. Target (eds) (2002) *Outcomes of Psychoanalytic Treatment*. London: Whurr.

Bick, J. (1985) Further considerations of the function of skin in early object relations, *British Journal of Psychotherapy*, 2(4): 292.

Bion, W. ([1962] 1984) *Learning from Experience*. London: Karnac.

Bion, W. (1965) *Transformations*. New York: Jason Aaronson.

Blanco, M. (1988) *Thinking, Feeling, and Being*. London: Routledge.

Blos, P. (1979) *The Adolescent Passage*. Madison: International Universities Press.

Bowlby, J. (1973) *Attachment and Loss*. Harmondsworth: Penguin.

Breuer, J. (1895) *Case Histories: 1. Fraulein Anna O*, in J. Strachey (ed.) (1955) *Standard Edition of the Complete Psychological Works of Sigmund Freud*, vol. 2, p. 21. London: Hogarth Press.

Breuer, J. and Freud, S. (1895) *Studies in Hysteria*, in J. Strachey (ed.) (1955) *Standard Edition of the Complete Psychological Works of Sigmund Freud*, vol. 2, p. 1. London: Hogarth Press.

Buber, M. ([1923] 1958) *I and Thou*. New York: Scribner.

Buckingham, L. (1994) Teaching Klein, *British Journal of Psychotherapy*, 11(2): 298.

Coltart, N. (1996) *The Baby and the Bathwater*. London: Karnac.

Cooper, M. (2003) *Existential Therapies*. London: Sage.

Coren, A. (2001) *Short Term Psychotherapy: A Psychodynamic Approach*. London: Karnac.

Cross, M. and Papadopoulos, R. (2001) *Becoming a Therapist*. London: BrunnerRoutledge.

Dalal, F. (2002) *Race, Colour and the Process of Racialisation*. London: BrunnerRoutledge.

Dickens, C. ([1859] 1997) *A Tale of Two Cities*, ed. W. Busch. New York: New American Library.

Dinnage, R. (1988) *One to One*. Harmondsworth: Penguin.

Dreher, A. (2002) *The Aims of Psychoanalytic Treatment*, in M. Leuzinger-Bohleber and M. Target (eds) *Outcomes of Psychoanalytic Treatment*. London: Whurr.

Elliot, T. S. (1942) Little Gidding, in T. S. Eliot (1963) *Collected Poems*. New York: Harcourt Brace.

Elton, B. (2000) *Inconceivable*. London: Black Swan.

Erikson, E. (1965) *Culture and Society*. Harmondsworth: Penguin.

Ferenczi, S. (1933) *Final Contributions to the Problems and Methods of Psychoanalysis*. London: Hogarth Press.

Fonagy, P. (2000) *What Works for Whom? A Critical Review of Treatments for Children and Adolescents*. New York: Guilford Press.

Freud, S. (1900) *The Interpretation of Dreams*, in J. Strachey (ed.) (1955) *Standard Edition of the Complete Psychological Works of Sigmund Freud*, vol. 4, p. 1, vol. 5, p. 39. London: Hogarth Press.

Freud, S. (1905) *Three Essays on the Theory of Sexuality: Chapter III*, The transformations of puberty, in J. Strachey (ed.) (1955) *Standard Edition of the Complete Psychological Works of Sigmund Freud*, vol. 7, p. 207. London: Hogarth Press.

Freud, S. (1909) *Notes upon a Case of Obsessional Neurosis*, in J. Strachey (ed.) (1955) *Standard Edition of the Complete Psychological Works of Sigmund Freud*, vol. 10, p. 158. London: Hogarth Press.

Freud, S. (1913) *On Beginning the Treatment*, in J. Strachey (ed.) (1955) *Standard Edition of the Complete Psychological Works of Sigmund Freud*, vol. 12, p. 121. London: Hogarth Press.

Freud, S. (1915) *Observations on Transference Love*, in J. Strachey (ed.) (1955) *Standard Edition of the Complete Psychological Works of Sigmund Freud*, vol. 12, p. 157. London: Hogarth Press.

Freud, S. (1932) *New Introductory Lectures on Psycho-analysis*, in J. Strachey (ed.) (1955) *Standard Edition of the Complete Psychological Works of Sigmund Freud*, vol. 22, p. 7. London: Hogarth Press.

Freud, S. (1939) *Moses and Monotheism*, in J. Strachey (ed.) (1955) *Standard Edition of the Complete Psychological Works of Sigmund Freud*, vol. 23, p. 7. London: Hogarth Press.

Gedo, J. and Goldberg, A. (1975) *Models of the Mind*. Chicago: Chicago University Press.

Gerard, J. (1999) Love in the time of psychotherapy, in D. Mann (ed.) *Erotic Transference and Countertransference*. London: Routledge.

GMC (General Medical Council) (2004) *Confidentiality: Protecting and Providing Information*. London: General Medical Council.

Goldberg, A. (1998) Deconstructing the dialectic, *International Journal of Psychoanalysis*, 79: 215.

Green, V. (2003) *Emotional Development, Psychoanalysis, Attachment Theory and Neuroscience*. London: BrunnerRoutledge.

Guimon, J. (2001) *Inequity and Madness*. New York: Kluwer Academic.

Haddon, M. (2003) *The Curious Incident of the Dog in the Night-time*. London: David Fickling Books.

Haley, J. (1976) *Problem-Solving Therapy*. New York: Harper & Row.

Harlow, H. F. (1958) Affectional response in the infant monkey, *Science*, 130: 421.

Haynes, J. and Miller, J. (eds) (2003) *Inconceivable Conceptions*. Hove: BrunnerRoutledge.

Haynes, J. and Wiener, J. (1996) The analyst in the counting house, *British Journal of Psychotherapy*, 13(1): 14.

Heidegger, M. ([1927] 1963) *Being and Time*. New York: Harper & Row.

Heimann, P. (1950) On counter transference, *International Journal of Psychoanalysis*, 31: 81.

Herman, N. (1988) *My Kleinian Home*. London: Free Association Books.

Hidas, G. (1993) 'Flowing over–transference, contertransference, telepathy: subjective dimensions of the psychoanalytic relationship in Ferenczi's thinking', in L. Aron and A. Harris (eds) *The Legacy of Sandor Ferenczi*. Hillsdale, NJ: Analytic Press.

Hill, J. (1993) 'Am I a Kleinian? Is anyone?' *British Journal of Psychotherapy*, 9(4): 463.

Hinshelwood, R. D. (1991) Psychodynamic formulation in assessment for psychotherapy, *British Journal of Psychotherapy*, 8(2): 166.

Hinshelwood, R. D. (1997) *Therapy or Coercion: Does Psychoanalysis Differ from Brainwashing?* London: Karnac.

Holmes, J. (1995) How I assess for psychoanalytic psychotherapy, in C. Mace (ed.) *The Art and Science of Assessment*. London: Routledge.

Hunter, M. and Struve, J. (1998) *The Ethical Use of Touch in Psychotherapy*. London: Sage.

Jackson, L. (2002) *Freaks, Geeks and Asperger's Syndrome: A User's Guide to Adolescence*. London: Jessica Kingsley.

Jones, J. (2002) *Terror and Transformation*. London: Routledge.

Kernberg, O. (1985) *Borderline Conditions and Pathological Narcissism*. NJ: Aronson.

King, P. (1980) 'The life cycle as indicated by the nature of the transference in the psychoanalysis of the middle aged and elderly', *International Journal of Psychoanalysis*, 61: 153.

Klauber, J. *et al.* (1987) *Illusion and Spontaneity in Psychoanalysis.* London: Free Association Books.

Klein, M. (1931) A contribution to the theory of intellectual inhibition, in M. Klein (1985) *Love, Guilt and Reparation.* London: Hogarth Press.

Klein, M. (1940) Mourning and its relation to manic depressive states, in M. Klein (1985) *Love, Guilt and Reparation.* London: Hogarth Press.

Klein, M. (1959) Our adult world and its roots in infancy, *Human Relations*, 12.

Knox, J. (2003) *Archetype, Attachment, Analysis.* London: Brunner-Routledge.

Kohut, H. (1965) *The Analysis of the Self.* New Haven, CT: International Universities Press.

Kubler Ross, E. (1973) *On Death and Dying.* London: Routledge.

Lacan, J. (1949) The mirror-stage as formative of the I as revealed in psychoanalytic experience, in J. Lacan (1977) *Écrits: A Selection.* New York: Norton.

Lacan, J. (1951) *Écrits*, in J. Mitchell and J. Rose (eds) (1982) *Feminine Sexuality.* New York: Norton.

Lacan, J. (1954) *Seminar 1* in J.-A. Miller (ed.) (1988) *The Seminar, Book I: Freud's Papers on Technique.* New York: Norton.

Lacan, J. (1955) *Seminar II* in J.-A. Miller (ed.) (1988) *The Seminar, Book II: The Ego in Freud's Theory and in the Technique of Psychoanalysis.* New York: Norton.

Lacan, J. (1956) *Seminar III* in J.-A. Miller (ed.) (1993) *The Seminar, Book III: The Psychoses.* New York: Norton.

Lacan, J. (1966) The direction of the treatment in *Écrits* (1988). London: Routledge.

Lacan, J. (1973) Of the subject who is supposed to know, in J. Lacan (1973) *The Four Fundamental Concepts of Psychoanalysis.* Harmondsworth: Penguin.

Laing, R. D. (1961) *Self and Others.* Harmondsworth: Penguin Books.

Lander, R. (2003) The incontinent analyst, *International Journal of Psychoanalysis*, 84(4): 691.

Lazarus, A. (1989) *The Practice of Multimodal Therapy.* Baltimore, MD: Johns Hopkins University Press.

Levinas, E. (1996) *Basic Philosophical Writing.* Bloomington, IN: Indiana University Press.

Livingston Smith, D. (1991) *Hidden Conversations.* London: Tavistock/ Routledge.

Lomas, P. (1987) *The Limits of Interpretation.* Harmondsworth: Penguin.

Luria, A.R. (1961) *The Role of Speech I: Normal and Abnormal Behaviour.* Oxford: Pergamon Press.

Maduro, R. (1987) The initial dream and analysability in beginning analysis, *Journal of Analytical Psychology*, 32: 199.

Malan, D. (1965) *Individual Psychotherapy and the Science of Psychodynamics*. London: Butterworth.

Malik, K. (1996) *Race: Race, History and Culture in Western Society*. London: Macmillan.

Mander, G. (2000) *A Psychodynamic Approach to Brief Therapy*. London: Sage.

Mannoni, M. (1987) *The Child, His Illness and the Other*. London: Karnac Books.

Mantel, H. (2003) Clinical waste, in J. Haynes and J. Miller (eds) *Inconceivable Conceptions*. London: BrunnerRoutledge.

Maroda, K. (1991) *The Power of Countertransference*. Chichester: Wiley.

Mitchell, J. (2003) *Siblings*. Cambridge: Polity Press.

Murdin, L. (2000) *How Much is Enough?* London: Routledge.

Ogden, T. (1992) *The Primitive Edge of Experience*. London: Karnac.

Olivier, C. (1989) *Jocasta's Children*. London: Routledge.

Orwell, G. (1990) *Nineteen Eighty Four*. Harmondsworth: Penguin.

Palomera, V. (1997) On counter transference, in B. Burgoyne and M. Sullivan (eds) *The Klein–Lacan Dialogues*. London: Rebus Press.

Papadopoulos, R. and Saayman, G. (eds) (1984) *Jung in Modern Perspective*. London: Wildwood House.

Racker, H. (1968) *Transference and Counter-transference*. London: Karnac.

Ragland, E. (1995) *Essays on the Pleasures of Death*. London: Routledge.

Raphael Leff, J. (2003) Eros and art, in J. Haynes and J. Miller (eds) *Inconceivable Conceptions*. London: BrunnerRoutledge.

Rogers, C. (1965) *Client Centred Therapy*. London: Constable.

Rose, J. (2000) Symbols and their function in managing the anxiety of change: an intersubjective approach, *International Journal of Psychoanalysis*, 81: 453.

Rowan, J. (2001) *Ordinary Ecstasy*. London: BrunnerRoutledge.

Rustin, M. (2001) *Reason and Unreason*. London: Continuum.

Rycroft, C. (1968) *Imagination and Reality*. London: Maresfield.

Rycroft, C. (1995) On beginning a treatment, *British Journal of Psychotherapy*, 11(4): 514.

Safran, J. and Muran, C. (2000) *Negotiating the Therapeutic Alliance*. New York: Guilford Press.

Saks, E. R. (2001) *Interpreting Interpretation*. New Haven, CT: Yale University Press.

Samuels, A. (1985) *Jung and the Post-Jungians*. London: Routledge.

Schore, A. (2003) The human unconscious: the development of the right brain and its part in human development, in V. Green (ed.) *Emotional Development in Psychoanalysis, Attachment Theory and Neuroscience*. Hove: BrunnerRoutledge.

Schumeli, A. (2003) *The role of personality factors and attachment status in the selection of psychodynamic therapists: a psychoanalytic approach.* Unpublished doctoral thesis.

Searles, H. (1959) Oedipal love in the countertransference in H. F. Searles *Collected Papers on Schizophrenia and Related Subjects.* London: Maresfield.

Segal, H. (1982) *Introduction to the Work of Melanie Klein.* London: Hogarth Press.

Smith, A. (1776) *An Inquiry into the Nature and Causes of the Wealth of Nations,* ed. E. Cana (1994). New York: Random House.

Sousa, P., Pineira, R. and Silva, R. (2003) Questions about questions, *International Journal of Psychoanalysis,* 84(4): 865.

Strachey, J. (1934) The nature of the therapeutic action of interpretation in psychoanalysis, *International Journal of Psychoanalysis,* 15: 117.

Strachey, J. (ed.) (1955) *Standard Edition of the Complete Psychological Works of Sigmund Freud.* London: Hogarth Press.

Suman, A. and Brignone, A. (2001) Transference, counter transference: society and culture before and during the first encounter, *British Journal of Psychotherapy,* 17(4): 465.

Symington, N. (1986) The analyst's act of freedom as agent of therapeutic change. in G. Kohon (ed.) *The British School of Psychoanalysis – The Independent Tradition.* London: Free Association Press.

Szasz, T. ([1972] 1984) *The Myth of Mental Illness.* New York: Harper & Row.

Tallis, F. (2002) *Hidden Minds.* London: Profile Books.

Tinbergen, N. (1951) *The Study of Instinct.* Oxford: Clarendon Press.

Totton, N. (2002) Foreign bodies: recovering the history of body psycho-therapy, in T. Staunton (ed.) *Body Psychotherapy.* London: Taylor & Francis.

Tracey, T. J. (1988) Relationship of responsibility attribution congruency to psychotherapy outcome, *Journal of Social and Clinical Psychology,* 7(2-2): 131.

Trowell, J. and Etchegoyen, A. (2002) *The Importance of Fathers.* London: Routledge.

Tuckwell, G. (2002) *Racial Identity, White Counsellors and Therapists.* Buckingham: Open University Press.

Tustin, F. (1986) *Autistic Barriers in Neurotic Patients.* New Haven, CT: Yale University Press.

Tustin, F. (1990) *The Protective Shell in Children and Adults.* London: Karnac Books.

United Kingdom Council for Psychotherapy (2004) *Ethical Requirements.* London: UKCP.

Van Deurzen, E. (2002) *Existential Counselling and Psychotherapy in Practice.* London: Sage.

Winnicott, D. (1935) The manic defence, in D. Winnicott (1992) *Through Paediatrics to Psychoanalysis*. London: Karnac.

Winnicott, D. (1960) 'Ego Distortion in terms of true and false self' in *The Maturational Processes and the Facilitating Environment*. London: Hogarth Press.

Winnicott, D. (1965) *The Maturational Processes and the Facilitating Environment*. London: Hogarth Press.

Winnicott, D. (1988) *Human Nature*. London: Free Association Books.

Zetzel, E. (1956) Current concepts of transference, *International Journal of Psychoanalysis*, 37: 369.

INDEX

167